PRAISE FOR G!

"Thank you, Scott, for w [...] importantly, I am grateful to [...] being guardians and loving parents. There is probably no mission in life more critical than supporting and raising a child. To ALL of you who go the life-changing, extra mile to be guardians and kinship care givers, *Guardian Shift* is a valuable resource for you! Thank you, Scott, for sharing your life to another generation and for sharing your experience here in *Guardian Shift*."

–JOHN SCIAMANNA, Vice President, Public Policy,
CHILD WELFARE LEAGUE OF AMERICA,
Washington, DC

"Although being a stepfather is not the same as being a guardian, the two are parallel. Having read Scott Amaral's *Guardian Shift*, I realize just how much it would have helped my journey. I highly recommend it to anyone considering becoming a guardian or marrying someone with children. It will definitely make your journey much smoother."

–BARRY S. GREENFIELD, Formerly of
ABC TV's GOOD MORNING AMERICA

"Scott Amaral's *Guardian Shift* is a much-needed deep dive into how grandparents and other relatives or family friends can manage when they take on the important task of raising others' children. Practical tips and insights from those who have journeyed this path make the book an excellent resource."

−AMY GOYER, Speaker, Consultant,
*Author of **Juggling Life, Work and Caregiving,***
AARP's Family and Caregiving Expert

"In today's world of broken families, there is a great need for *Guardian Shift*. This book will be a blessing to anyone entering into unexpected guardianship of a child and to single-parents faced with future-planning for their children should a loss occur. Most of all, *Guardian Shift* will be a blessing to the children whose guardians are in desperate need of a guide that can chauffeur them through this new life. Amaral provides invaluable real-world examples, support and resources for any family facing the reality of a guardian shift."

−MO ANDESON, Vice Chairman of the Board
KELLER WILLIAMS REALTY INTERNATIONAL
*Author of **A Joy-Filled Life***

"Scott Amaral's Guardian Shift offers practical advice, lived-experience, encouragement, and information for those raising their relative's children. This book fills a gap in the growing support network for kinship families."

−KIM STEVENS, M.ED., Program Director
NORTH AMERICAN COUNCIL ON
ADOPTABLE CHILDREN

"*Guardian Shift* is a welcome resource perfect for anyone who has taken on the important role of caring for another's child. The short, easy-to-read chapters target many of the joys and challenges which guardians experience and provide practical resources for support. Full of touching personal stories from Scott Amaral and other guardians, the reader will immediately feel as if they have connected with a friend who understands."

–ALISON CALIENDO, M.A.,Executive Director
at FOSTER KINSHIP

"I applaud Scott Amaral for bringing us *Guardian Shift*! It's a good wake-up call for everyone to help look after the needs of guardian parents. We live in a day when so many children are suddenly left alone and in need of family members to step up with love and support. As grandparents who have shared the rearing of a grandchild ourselves, my wife and I recommend this book in support of those who are raising other people's children."

–IRV BROWN, Grandparent, Police Chaplain

"Scott has practical suggestions for current and prospective guardians as they navigate through this process. From his passionate writing, Scott motivates and promotes others to be life changers by creating nurturing "shifts." His aim is to encourage and empower others by offering the insights he has gathered from his own experience and those from other guardians."

–DIANE ASHMORE, MS, LMFT,
Licensed Marriage, and Family Therapist

"With the growing number of kinship families, we need more resources like Amaral's *Guardian Shift*."

–GIANNA DAHLIA, Executive Director
at TOGETHER WE RISE, Brea, CA
"Every day, 1,200 Kids enter foster care in the United States. Together We Rise is a non-profit that changes the way they experience the system."

"My life has been changed and my soul altered, as a mother, as a professional, and as I have come to know and hear the hearts of Scott and Jeannie Amaral. You are a blessing for becoming a guardian. May you be blessed on your journey. *Guardian Shift* is one of those special gifts for you!"

–LAURA W. BOYD, Ph.D.,
National Child Welfare Consultant
FAMILY FOCUS TREATMENT ASSOCIATION

"In a world where life imitates art and more children are in need of a teacher like Mr. Miyagi, a mentor like Obi-Wan, and a loving father figure like Uncle Phil. *Guardian Shift* takes an excellent approach guiding people through the many different stages of guardianship that many often find themselves in unexpectedly. Through the joys and pitfalls of the journey, you will be blessed with Scott's experience and insight."

–LITO SOLORIO, Teaching Pastor at
NORTHSIDE CHRISTIAN CHURCH, Clovis, Ca

"As a single mom... I want to thank you, Scott, for writing **Guardian Shift**! In fact, I put the book into my safety deposit box with my will. I had recently spoken to a friend about my motherly worry of guardianship for my children should the Lord bring me home before they are adults. This book is truly needed for many!"

–KELLIE CLARK, Single Mother

"Scott Amaral's **Guardian Shift** is the perfect resource for the countless caregivers who take on the scary, yet rewarding, journey of guardianship. The book provides excellent insight and practical tips to help understand the kinship care experience, and fills a void for guardians who often have nowhere to turn for help."

–TIFFANY ALLEN, Senior Associate
CHILD FOCUS, INC.
Innovative consultants connecting people,
programs and policy to cutting-edge child welfare,
kinship care and other child advocacy issues.
DC, Maryland, Rhode Island

ENCOURAGEMENT & INSPIRATION FOR

GUARDIAN
SHIFT

GRANDPARENTS, AUNTS, UNCLES &
ANYONE RAISING OTHER PEOPLE'S CHILDREN

SCOTT AMARAL

The Library of Congress Cataloging-in-Publication Data
is on file with the Library of Congress,
Washington, DC.
LCCN: 2016914528

ISBN-10: 1-62747-297-5
ISBN-13: 978-1-62747-297-5

Printed in the United States of America

Guardian Shift is dedicated to encouraging and inspiring those of you raising children in guardianship, formally or informally.

Guardian Shift is also dedicated to the people who are close to you, whom I call your "Support People." They play an important role in your family's well-being.

Thank you for caring for the world's next generation!

"THE BETTER THE LIVES OF GUARDIANS, THE BETTER THE CHILDREN'S LIVES ARE IN GUARDIANSHIP."
Scott Amaral, Guardian Shift

Contents

Foreword

Children change our lives and alter our souls. Many, if not all of us, made an overt, public decision of marriage that included "for better or for worse." This vow was entered into – supposedly – deliberately and freely. When it comes to raising our children, parents typically enter a similar commitment, even if entered one-sided only.

Yet families have changed. And changed dramatically! No longer is the grandparent-led family an anomaly. Society recruits and appreciates foster families, who volunteer to care for a child in need of a family. Cities and towns have laws establishing "safe harbors," where an unwanted infant can be left safe and without retaliation against the birth parent(s).

But what if that "bundle of joy" comes to you in the form of a nine year old, or a fifteen year old, or via telephone from state child welfare or juvenile delinquency representatives? What if that child, regardless of gender or age, is acutely depressed, drug-involved, sex-trafficked, or acting out his or her trauma with angry outbursts or stealing or inappropriate language and sexual displays? AND what if that child has no one else to care for, guide, or assume parental authority for him or her?

Welcome to the world of guardianship! Of course, since you have picked up this book, you know the challenge. And you are probably anxious for as much support, encouragement, and understanding as you can grab from the words and pages that you are about to delve into.

Guardianship means that you are now responsible, whether your ward is a blood relative or not. Voluntary? That's the rub! Yes, you chose to enter into this legal arrangement, yet hardly by free will and volition. Something has gone wrong – maybe terribly wrong – and you have decided you must step in and step up. Was there a death? A substance-abuse problem? A relative with serious physical or mental illness? Or a relative with horrible decision making, whose choices put others at risk?

What is it that you are feeling? Is it love? Hope? Optimism? Anger? Resentment? Fear? Guilt? All of those?

Here is your invitation to *Guardian Shift.* You need to identify with real people who have traveled this path, and you need practical ideas to address real problems such as setting relationships and boundaries, dealing with other family members, establishing a new family identity, and yes, social media.

The words of Scott Amaral, with commentary from his wife, Jeannie, provide the guidance and those specific, practical suggestions. You will feel his passion for the commitment you have made to your family. You will also experience his praise for making this journey. As Scott says: "You're the glue that holds a hurting generation together, providing them a future."

I have spent my professional life of four decades committed to children and families: as a public school teacher, as a therapist, as an elected official, and as a national child-welfare consultant. Yet where I learned the most about life and about myself was not in any of those arenas, as rich in growth experiences as they were.

My greatest learning and my proudest accomplishment is that of "mother." Like you, I did not always, in hindsight, respond as I wish I had. I certainly was smart enough to know I needed to learn more! Fortunately, I had friends with children, all along the way, at whatever ages my own children were. There were also books to read and magazines to subscribe to. I had access to internet articles galore to address almost any challenge or question... or simply to offer a creative opportunity.

And like you, I have both been blessed by and endured difficult times: marriage, childbirth, adoption, guardianship, cancer, loss of a relationship, financial loss, and professional acclaim as well as professional disappointment. Thank goodness for any and all resources I found along the way.

Guardian Shift is a resource just for you, the guardian – although its wisdom and healing words also apply for all of you mothers, fathers, step-parents, foster parents and single parents. *Guardian Shift* is a unique gift for all of you making a difference in the next generation of raising other people's children!

Each chapter is a short read, yet it is emotionally universal to the guardianship experience. Each chapter includes a Recap of wisdom that is uplifting and practical. It is a necessary resource for you – a large population of guardians for whom there has been little recognition, voice, or support.

My life has been changed and my soul altered, as a mother and as a professional, as I have come to know and hear the hearts of Scott and Jeannie Amaral. You, dear reader, are a blessing for becoming a guardian. May you be blessed on your journey.

Guardian Shift is one of those special gifts for you!

Laura W. Boyd, Ph.D.
National Child Welfare Consultant
Family Focus Treatment Association

Preface

There are many reasons I was motivated to write *Guardian Shift*. The foremost reason was that in 2008, when our guardianship concluded, my wife Jeannie and I searched the internet for some encouragement. Finding little available at that time was very disappointing. Therefore, my attention quickly turned to creating something helpful for others who are guardians, or who are contemplating the difficult role of guardianship.

This has been a labor of love – with multiple goals in mind – written to encourage and build awareness for this overlooked form of parenting. I charted my course by talking to many other guardians, and gathered useful information, which I now am pleased to share with you. *Guardian Shift* also has a lot to offer to those who are close to the guardians – our "Support People." They are like our own personal angels for parenting in guardianship, and their role is extremely important because they help us through tough times. Having that person to talk to, and understanding the new family dynamic, is extremely valuable.

It was at the time when our guardianship concluded, that I committed to bring *Guardian Shift* to you. You are the most important people in the lives of the next generation, and you need to be encouraged. Parenting other people's children in guardianship, whether the arrangement is formal or informal, is a noble gift to the future of our world. May *Guardian Shift* bring you encouragement and inspiration!

Introduction

Current studies show that in the United States, approximately 8 million children live in guardianship,[1] either formal or informal. Aunts, uncles and grandparents raise nieces, nephews and grandchildren. This also includes those of you who are not even related to the children you are raising. *Guardian Shift* offers practical advice and tips to all of you brave souls who are raising the next generation.

This form of parenting is unique, though it has similarities to both foster care and adoption. The struggles that all these families go through are highly emotional. The current support system for families parenting children in guardianship is slim to none. It's a strong possibility that you may even know someone who is currently being raised or was raised by their grandparents or another relative.

This is the first book in the *Guardian Shift* series. It will be the platform for building awareness across the country, encouraging and inspiring families through the challenges of their journey in guardianship. In the following pages, you will discover how emotional struggles and battles are addressed, an issue that guardians face every day. These can range widely – from feelings of being stepped on by other family members, to the joy that guardians feel in making that positive change, and providing a future to those in their care. There has also been a tremendous shift in the lives of children in guardianship as they adjust to having a different adult raising them. They now find themselves in a totally new living situation, and the challenges for all involved are immense.

Guardian Shift also takes a look at the balancing act of integrating the new family member(s) with your own biological children. In this book I will also call guardians together, creating a platform. It will unite aunts, uncles, grandparents, unrelated guardians – anyone raising other people's children – to join and engage with one another to provide mutual encouragement. I have also included real-life stories from guardians, and adults who were raised in guardianship, throughout the book.

Those of you raising the next generation will benefit from the strategies outlined in *Guardian Shift*. They range from the "Honeymoon Phase" to the "Finishing Well" stage of your guardianship. You will be able to identify, and understand, that the path of guardianship can be much bigger than you may have first thought. You will discover that you are not the only one dealing with lonely and isolated feelings. I am hopeful that the millions who are on this journey of guardianship will find a way to use social media to connect. I extend an invitation to you to do so, at any time before you finish reading this book. *Guardian Shift* brings real-life solutions to the daily struggles that affect us all.

Family and friends of guardians in the midst of this parenting style – our "Support People" – will greatly benefit from reading about what their loved ones are going through. They are the key support people to both the guardians and the children in their care. This book will give them a deeper insight into how they can become better at providing support to your family. May *Guardian Shift* bring you the encouragement and inspiration that you so richly deserve.

Section One

Your Shifting World

As I was contemplating how taking children in under guardianship affects our lives, it compelled me to address several areas. In this first section, "Your Shifting World," the goal is multifaceted for those of you who are parenting other people's children. Millions are on this journey, and the perceptions of those who don't understand what you are going through can be daunting. We're going to show how those who are close to you can become better support people. Guardianship is a highly overlooked form of parenting, and the hurts and complications involved in it are plentiful.

I hope to help you find the encouragement you need, and to help you discover why you're the best person for the task. You could be holding on to the possibility that you don't feel you are equipped for this shift in your world. Stay with me as we look to overcome this feeling. I will help you find your identity as a new guardian, or refresh it as a seasoned one – a truly important role – whether your guardian role began at the early age of nineteen or you are a grandparent raising a child in your eighties. You're the glue that holds a hurting generation together, providing them with a future. Enjoy this fresh perspective – and may it enrich your life!

Chapter One

The Shift Begins

I am so excited that this book has made it into your hands! As we spend time together here, I will do my very best to make this time as beneficial to you as possible. Once you're done, please take note of my invitation at the end of this book to continue our connection. Let's get started!

Wherever you are in your journey, it is my goal to enable you to do your best. Writing this book has been a long process for me. It began in 2003, before I ever knew I would write this book for you. I know much more now than I did then. Back then, Jeannie and I had a strong concern for our nephew, and we wanted to help him. I am going to assume that this is where you are in your journey, too. I presume that it is your desire to love and protect the child in your care. This should be the most important part of your commitment, as you step into this new parenting role.

There are various circumstances that may have brought you to your new position. Regardless of how your guardianship role came about, my heart goes out to you. Today it is more crucial than ever to pay special attention to those who will become our leaders in the future — our children. Since the 1960s, our culture has seen a decline within the family unit. Any psychologist will quickly convince you of a family crisis in America, as well as in other parts of the world. The assumption is that all of this stems from the dysfunction of today's shifting family values. Those who have put you in the position of becoming a guardian are mostly unaware of the damage they have caused. For example, they have now put you into the role of caring for other family members — traumatized children with emotional issues and much more. Some of you though, I must say, are now in this position because of a tragic event. You may have experienced an irreversible loss, from which you will never recover. If so, I am deeply sorry, and I offer my sympathies. However, your new commitment reveals your love and concern for another individual. It truly demonstrates your willingness to give, and to share your heart and your resources. Finding yourself in this new path puts you on a course that you may have never anticipated. For now, though, we are not going to dwell on how each of you became guardians – but together we're going to look at how to survive the struggles, and we'll also offer suggestions for success.

Today it is more crucial than ever to pay special attention to those who will become our leaders in the future — our children.

28

Caring for children in guardianship is a huge calling. When you bring another child into your home to raise, you experience a multitude of challenges. The "Shift" into being a guardian does not come with a training manual. It may have been thrust upon you, or you may have been the one to take the initiative yourself. The family drama that may have erupted to cause the "Guardian Shift" is unique for every family, but there are similarities. However you came about it, you are now called as a guardian – and your job is to guard.

If you are reading this as a parent contemplating guardianship, this excites me! You may find a perspective in these pages of how things flow and this could protect another young life. If this is you, we want to say, don't wait to protect – just go and help that child, and keep reading this book. The sooner we get these little ones (sometimes not-so-little ones) into a better environment, the better off they will be. Guardianship is an intimidating task, and one that needs to be a long-term commitment. Take in all you can while you are turning these pages.

> *The "Shift" into being a guardian does not come with a training manual.*

Guardian Shift is designed with short chapters. I understand that you don't have the time to read a novel on the topic; rather, you need to be able to finish a section with ease. Respecting your time, I tried to keep the chapters somewhat brief (although this first chapter is a bit lengthy). ***Guardian Shift*** will give you points to consider and allow you to implement them quickly as they apply to your own family. Sometimes, when you become a guardian, you don't have much reaction time available, and you must make immediate decisions. This book will have lots of subjects related to your journey, depending on the age of your child. For example, we took in a fourteen-year-old boy, the next five years were tough, but every age and situation is different. You may take in a fourteen-year-old and have a marvelous time, so don't be scared off by the child's age if you are considering guardianship. Just remember that if a child is on your heart, it probably means you need to do something about it. No matter what age the child is, you can do it. I have met many adult children of guardianship, and they are truly grateful to have had someone take them in. Most, however, don't truly become grateful until later in life. This can be frustrating in the midst of your guardianship.

As you get a feel for my passion on the topic of raising children in guardianship, and my not-so-great sense of humor, I hope to become your new friend. Without a friend to commiserate with, who understands the spot you are now in, the role can sometimes be a bit tough. Your friends may say nice things to encourage you, but they just don't know the pair of shoes you walk in. Jeannie and I had some good friends – and believe me, they truly were great – but not too many could actually relate to the life-cycle we were in. This is okay – I never expected them to – but we were always grateful for their encouragement. Most people think of parenting in guardianship, and relate it quickly to foster care or adoption. This is a common misconception. Although these different forms of parenting have many similarities, there are many differences among them. Millions of people know someone

> *You are doing society a great favor with the work you do as a guardian.*

who has been raised by a family member, but can't imagine the inner workings of it all. By this, I mean the things that the family goes through. But stay tuned, because I've included a section for family and friends. It will give them the depth they need to really come to your aid – and if they read the entire book, you will have a newfound power partner!

I will also cover what I call the "in-laws" and the "out-laws" of guardianship. This is an area that wears many faces, and they seem to know just what type of guardian you should be. They will also tell you your mistakes before you have a moment to correct them. I hope to give you enough relatable scenarios to overcome their criticism, and to take control of your guardianship.

It is my commitment to cover the multitudes of issues we endure as guardians. This is my top priority. But there is one thing that has to be covered first – and it's how grateful I am to all of you! As a parent, having children in this world, I am grateful for those of you who protect the parentless. You are doing society a great favor with the work you do as a guardian. I mean it! You are tops! Okay, I know you could be thinking, "Why is Scott saying this?" Well, let me explain why I am so grateful. If you were *not* protecting the child in your charge as a guardian, who would be? What would society be like if you were not instilling good, solid values in this child? *This* is why I am expressing the gratitude that Jeannie and I feel toward you. The world is a better place because of you! Do those of us who are guardians ever make a mistake? YES! We do make mistakes – we do get blinded in our efforts to make a difference – but these children are in a better place because of us!

31

It's an honor for me to be writing these words to you. You're the reason that a child will go to bed with dinner and clean sheets. Being a guardian is not to be taken lightly! I am so very proud that I live in a world where people will stand up and fight to protect children who don't have parents of their own to protect and love them. The work you do, all wrapped in love, is bigger than you could ever imagine! So not for a moment – at least not while you are reading this book – are you to ever feel down, or to regret how your journey as a guardian is unfolding. I want you to feel as important to your guardian child as the sun is to the Earth, or as water is to a newly planted seed. My goal is to improve your belief in yourself. If I were the one being raised by you, I would want you to be strong. I would want to know that you are there for me. I might not have realized it at first, but one day – as a child of guardianship – I would understand.

You're special, and you must not downplay being a guardian. Understand that you are the very life support of the child in your care – and no one else is there to play that role! So, how important does this make you? Out of all the people in the world, *you* have become the guardian of the child in your care! So, in *my* book, this makes you the best of the best! This is how I will refer to you all the way through this book. No one else took the risk – but *you* did! I know how much you have gone through. Jeannie and I have been in your shoes, and it's not the easiest place to be – but it is certainly rewarding! We want you to know that we have the highest level of respect for you. We want to hear from you – and we want to get to know every one of you.

As we move into the topics that affect us as guardians, I want you to know that I will not have all the answers. I will never presume to know it all. That is not my goal here. My goal is to encourage you, and to network with you. I am here to express my heart for you in a sincere and authentic manner, and to help make each day in your journey a bit brighter. Here's my hope: to see **Guardian Shift** create the wind under your sails and give you the strength to achieve another milestone. This would be so exciting! I would burst at the seams if even *one* guardian was touched enough by this book not to give up – and because of this, one more child was protected! These are the goals of my writings. I am a father of four, and I also raised a nephew in guardianship. Jeannie and I know that if what I write to you touches you and brightens your day – then we have done our job!

Jeannie and I are just regular people. We're ordinary parents who want to encourage others who are raising children in guardianship. If you need to have intense professional help, I encourage you to seek it. This is the best advice I can give. You are on a journey that is unique to you, and I am not *ever* going to claim that this book will solve everyone's needs. You have become a guardian – which means that you are there to guard! Let's put it this way. Guardians, quite simply, are called to guard and protect! No further definition is needed. You're the guard. No one passes the gates without checking in with the guard, right? I am in Puerto Vallarta, Mexico, as I am writing this book to you. Jeannie and I live in a community that has 24 / 7 security. Not even our friends can get in to see us without the guard making sure that we know they're coming, and that we're expecting them. So, just as *I* am grateful to my security guard for holding the line of protection for *our* home, *you* are the guard to the child in your care, holding the line of protection for *your* home and making the child feel secure. You're the one who creates security for your child. Stand firm. You are the 24 / 7 guard at the security gate – never forget it! No one should ever get in and disrupt the work you do as a guardian. I want to be incredibly clear how this feels to your child. They may not acknowledge it at first, but they will feel it in their heart before their brain registers it. Hopefully, one day, their mouth will utter words of thanks to you. If you have been fortunate to hear words of gratitude already, then I am excited for you! For those who feel neglected in this area, I will stand in the gap for you here, with this book. I am telling you how grateful *I* am to you, for those you poured your life into!

Chapter Recap

So it can be said, "Guardians are Guards!" This must be the baseline we all use. If not, we run the risk of being trampled on by those who want to break into our world without permission. Live up to your title, and guard those in your charge! Remember: a child's life depends on you! Don't *ever* allow anyone who comes in for an attack to weaken you. And *never* give the attackers any credit for telling you what to do – it is *always* up to you. Hold strong! The child in your care may not thank you now, but chances are that they eventually will. Remember what your heart told you when you took guardianship of your child. It told you, "I must protect and make a difference." This affirmation now fuels your journey!

Chapter Two

Millions Are on This Journey

When Jeannie and I first started down our path of parenting our nephew in guardianship, we did not know any other aunts and uncles who had taken in a niece or nephew. We felt we were kind of out of the ordinary. In our little world, and even in the church we were attending, we found only one other family that were guardians – grandparents who were raising their grandson. In our circle of friends, and among other people we knew, we felt quite uncommon by adding our nephew to our household. In 2003, it was not as common, or as easy, to jump on the internet to research the subject of guardianship as it is today. I have to say, we found our guardianship attorney by a word-of-mouth campaign.

In the entire time we raised our nephew, we did not meet anyone else who had taken on this form of parenting. We felt very unique and isolated. In 2009, we found some stats called the "Grandfacts,"[1] which blew us away as to how many grandparents were raising their grandchildren. This marked the time we felt it was necessary to become advocates for those who stand in the gap of raising other people's children. Fast forward to 2011, when an AARP article by Marian Wright Edelman reported that *millions* of children are living in guardianship, formally or informally.[2] The numbers continue to grow, even though many of the children are "aging out" and no longer being counted. With these statistics showing this increase in children ending up in the care of others, it indicates that the family unit as we once knew it is declining. This, therefore, makes the notion of parenting children in guardianship the "new normal."

Your journey of becoming a guardian is unique to you. This holds so true, as we continue to connect with many of you and learn about you through your personal stories. Poverty, crime, drugs and the lack of parenting skills are all factors that contribute to the growing number of children who find themselves without suitable parents. I guess one could ask, "Where did it all start to break down?" I think that it breaks at different spots for each situation. One might say, "It's all the drugs," or "It's the lack of suitable jobs," and most of us would be right. It breaks in places that we just can't see sometimes – until a child becomes at risk. I am confident that you and I can make

> *Poverty, crime, drugs and the lack of parenting skills are all factors that contribute to the growing number of children who find themselves without suitable parents.*

a huge difference in the lives of these children. The faster we can respond to the children's needs, the sooner we can minimize their loss of family structure.

Fully understanding the huge number of children and adults involved in this form of parenting shocked us at first. Many of you may be shocked as well. We also found a much more alarming issue regarding those who weren't in a legal guardianship role, who wanted to be supportive to guardians, but who found themselves hesitant to get involved. The more adults who will come alongside you and support you in this process, the more you will feel the confidence and reassurance to keep going. In the many conversations I had with guardians, when they shared their biggest issues, they stated that the most common one they face is how their family and friends truly don't understand what they have committed to. They simply don't comprehend what has happened to their family dynamics. When your family and close friends have a better understanding, your life becomes much smoother. I have personally felt the impact of supportive people at the onset of our guardianship, and during the following five years of our teenage nephew's care.

In Generations United's 2013 report,[4] they estimate that families of guardianship save American taxpayers over $6.5 billion per year!

Another study conducted by Generations United[3] in 2013 showed similar statistics, with millions of children now living in what is commonly called a "grandfamily." These are families composed of grandparents, aunts and uncles who are raising grandchildren, nieces and nephews. This is a staggering number of children – some involved with the welfare system; others not.

Those adults who have the resources to obtain legal guardianship may be able to get benefits for the children. Others are struggling to put food on the table. They could never say no to providing a home for their own flesh and blood, no matter what kind of a strain it put on them. These families are all truly heroes in the sight of the children they care for.

We need more qualified families to rise up, more than ever, to care for these children who are at such great risk.

Few families have enough resources to care for additional family members. We were able to obtain legal guardianship for our nephew, which allowed him access to our medical plan. This is not always the case. Families in guardianship – formal or informal – take on huge expenses, which most will never recover from. Hopes of a golden retirement are dashed forever. In younger families, in the case of aunts and uncles, they are often blending families together, thus pulling time and money from their own biological children. In Generations United's 2013 report,[4] they estimate that families of guardianship save American taxpayers over $6.5 billion per year!

Many of these families are not interested in having the taxpayers of this nation pay the way for these children, but some have no choice. It is my goal to build awareness for all of these families. Personal friendships are so necessary for guardians during these times. Some guardians feel ashamed that a son, daughter, brother or sister took a direction that left them holding the bag in raising their children. The millions of households in the USA – or the world, for that matter – suffer a great deal on many levels, with the main ones being emotional and financial pain.

The need to raise other people's children will persist and grow as long as we have drug abuse and a lack of family values. Families that stand in the gap to care for these children are getting older, and in a few short generations this need could really get out of hand. Our country's grandparents are aging, and the values they have today may not be the same for the next generation of grandparents. What I mean is that the next generation of grandparents may not have learned the values they need to be successful at raising *their* grandchildren. If society continues to break down, the burden will fall on the foster-care system at an ever greater percentage every year. We need more qualified families to rise up, more than ever, to care for these children who are at such great risk. It will take people with strong family values to step up and protect these children. It is a critical calling to care for these children.

Chapter Recap

Every child who comes into an at-risk position needs a guardian to care for them. Those of you who stand in the gap are truly great people to step up and protect your guardian child. Know that you are not alone – and please don't feel shame in reaching out to others for some help. Many people actually would love to help, but don't understand how. Keep in mind that it's good to share your situation with those close to you, and let them help you along the way. Once people around you, namely your "Support People," have learned of your new role as a guardian, and how they can actually come alongside you to help, your life will smooth out. Hand them a copy of **Guardian Shift** as a gift – it will really become a gift not just to them, but also to you yourself – and to the child in your care!

Chapter Three

Defining Roles

When our guardianship unfolded in 2003, we found that many people were simply unaware of the type of arrangement we had made to parent our nephew. We found ourselves doing more explaining than we would have liked to. Fortunately, people we spoke to were more than supportive, once they understood our new role as guardians. You may not have experienced this. This experience, however, became our inspiration to bring more awareness to others, about guardianship, for all of us who are raising other people's children.

If you are a support person, rather than a guardian, this chapter is for you. It is designed to help those around you who may be parenting children in guardianship. Let's take some time to focus on this section, so that we can help friends and acquaintances fully understand this form of parenting. Having support people is truly essential to those who are parenting as guardians. You have no idea! You wonderful people bring inspiration to our souls as we deal with the web of emotions that conflict us daily. Support people are the glue holding our tired brains together when we guardians feel like quitting. They keep us going when we feel as if we may have brought a war into our family's home. More on the war later... but in the meantime, let's get as many of you fired up as we can – about being a guardian yourself, or a support to one!

In general, once people understand the difference, they become your biggest cheerleaders. I believe it is at the core of each human being to either protect a child or encourage someone who is doing so. I can't ever remember anyone, after they understood why we were raising our nephew, ever saying that this was not a worthwhile effort in life. It was more like admiration, and lifting us up on a pedestal. We were never looking for recognition, but, like many of you, merely doing what we knew needed to be done. *Guardian Shift's* goal is to lift those of you who are in the midst of parenting a child in guardianship — those who are contemplating a guardianship role — or who are, or have been a guardian at some point in your life. Helping you to recognize and encourage you is the main event here – then uniting all those I can, follows as a close second.

Having support people is truly essential to those who are parenting as guardians. You have no idea!

I have put together a short explanation of the differences among guardianship, foster care and adoption. These should help others understand you more clearly. It's a quick way to show the variations, and the challenges that you all face. It is intended to help you

46

lovingly explain how you are pulled in so many directions in this form of parenting. It may read a bit formally at first, but you can break it down into easier pieces. I think the biggest difference is that guardians have to deal personally with people, for example the biological parents, grandparents, cousins or in-laws, and the potential new "out-laws." They all want a say in telling you what to do. This section on helping others understand the differences will hopefully let people know the vast number of people that YOU deal with. It's not limited only to the social worker, the police department, the family counselor and the others you work with while trying to maintain balance in your life.

A child typically falls into the foster care system due to the lack of a creditable family member who is able to take in the child.

Guardianship

Court-appointed guardians assume the responsibility for both the physical and financial needs of the child. Guardians are typically a close relative of the child: grandparents, aunts and uncles. In most cases the guardians have an emotional interest in the child.

As guardian parent, you can face overwhelming challenges in blending the guardian parent role with raising your own family. In many cases, for example, the birth parents of the guardian child can make it difficult for the guardian parents and the child under guardianship.

Foster Care

A minor child becomes a part of the foster care system as a ward of the state. Then the minor child can be placed in a private home, which is operated by a state-certified caregiver referred to as a "foster parent. "A child typically falls into the foster care system due to the lack of a creditable family member who is able to take in the child.

Many children, on their path to adulthood, may be placed in multiple homes, one after another. Fortunately, some of these placements result in adoption, creating a permanent foundation for the foster child.   In the Foster Care situation, the foster parent is compensated by the state for their services.

Adoption

Adoption is a process whereby a person assumes the full responsibility for the parenting of a child. All rights and responsibilities from the biological parents are terminated. Unlike guardianship or foster care, adoption is intended to effect a permanent change in parental status. Adoptive parents usually have no interaction with the former (usually biological) family or extended family, unless they decided it would be an "open" adoption.

Adoption is a great way to create a permanent family. Many we know of have chosen international adoptions, it can be very costly, yet rewarding at the same time. Adopting within the USA can also be very costly, although you don't have the travel time and expenses involved with international adoption. Adoption, many times, will result through Foster Care or guardians adopting their grandchild, niece or nephew.

Chapter Recap

Understanding the differences among foster care, adoption and guardianship is crucial to your social and family balance. Once others know what you are going through, they can better assist and encourage you. The more support people you have in your life, the more quality of life you will have. People want to come alongside you and help, once they understand. I want to encourage you to find the ones who are safe, let them know how they can best support you, and let them in.

Please understand my heart here. I am grateful for ALL parents in ALL forms of parenting! Without those who support the foster care system, in each of its aspects, we all would be in a world of hurt. Foster parenting is not only noble in and of itself, it sometimes leads to adoption! There are many people who would love to adopt one or more children and provide the love and nurturing they so need. My goal for parents of guardianship is to gain the same type and amount of attention and support that foster care and adoption, thankfully, already have!

Chapter Four

Hurting from the Sidelines

Our journeys as guardians all start in unique ways. For many of you they start very slowly, as nieces and nephews and grandchildren are born into this world. This situation is different, because deep in our souls we sometimes see the potential problem from afar. As we watch the new life come into the world, we may already see family issues arising. For Jeannie and me, however, it was *very unexpected,* as we learned of our nephew, and his situation, mostly by surprise. We received a phone call from someone we knew who worked in medical records at the local hospital — and who informed us that we might have a nephew. This person encouraged us to come to the hospital, and meet the mother and child.

My wife Jeannie shares, in her own words, about the first time we met our nephew...

After the call, we headed right down to the hospital to meet our new nephew and the baby's mother. We found our way up to the labor and delivery floor and located the new mother. She seemed delighted to meet us after I explained my relationship to the baby's father. She was happy to introduce her newborn son. Our own firstborn son was just five and a half months old at the time, so we were expecting to see a similar baby – pink, plump and healthy looking. However, our hearts were touched and saddened when we first saw our little nephew. He was very skinny, his skin was a gray, ashen color and he looked generally unhealthy. Where was that healthy "new-baby glow"? With a little more conversation with his mom, we discovered that she was a smoker and had not discontinued the habit during pregnancy. We are not sure if that was the only factor that had contributed to his unhealthy appearance, but we left it as such.

He was looking at going home with his aunt and uncle that night, to live with his three cousins, or going to juvenile hall. It was going to be his choice.

This was just the introduction to what would become years of hurting. As time went on, we followed the story of our nephew, but we never really got to see him much. Then one day our nephew's father obtained full custody of him. This came after the little guy rolled down a flight of stairs. His journey seemed to be clearing up and stabilizing, until the father's drug abuse landed our nephew on the streets, following the path his father had.

We hurt a great deal over the years, and much of the hurt I won't include in this book. The main point of this section is for people to know that this was no quick weekend decision. As *you* considered your options to take guardianship of the child in *your* care, I imagine it happened slowly and painfully. This is a lot to take in – watching and attempting to help the biological parents be better parents can be gut-wrenching. So when you or I end up in a guardianship role, most likely it didn't just happen overnight, as some may think. There are, however, those who lost parents tragically – and in this case you *did* become guardians overnight. You became the instant go-to person. This is a heartbreaking situation, and a very difficult one, because you or the child in your care had a paradigm shift in a split second. This is a topic that my own mother and father dealt with, as their two nieces and two nephews, although grown at the time, lost their parents to a train collision. My parents, their aunt and uncle, became the matriarch and patriarch for them and their children. A tradition was born for Easter, where all of these children and their children would come to our house every year for a big Easter gathering. This was, of course, not limited to Easter alone, but many other occasions over the years. For those of you who became instant guardians, I have a special connection to how you may have arrived at this point – or, should I say, a way to relate to you too!

It's a bit odd that I would be able to relate from both angles, but I am glad I can. Being raised around my older cousins, whom I looked up to, was cool. It was as though my parents had given me a bigger perspective, with four additional older "siblings" enlarging our family. I think that this prepared my heart to respond to the guardianship call, without my consciously

> *Guilt never produces a positive outcome. You need to grab hold of it and toss it out the window as often as it pops its ugly head up. Guilt will only keep you from making good choices in your guardianship role.*

knowing it. I didn't have to think more than a second to step up to the plate and take Jeannie's nephew in. It hurt our whole family as we watched our nephew lead a life so different from that of our sons, but we had very little say in the matter. Can you relate? If so, it is a painful process, and many don't realize this.

As you watched, my guess is that your heart was breaking – and this caused you a time of silent anger. I can feel your pain level going up in my soul as I write this sentence. I am sure that when you took on the objective to protect the child now in your care, you must have tried proper reasoning first, to resolve the protection of the child. For those who tried reasoning to no avail, there was the legal system. We "watched from the sidelines" until we finally had enough and went after him – and it wasn't easy! At age fourteen, he hadn't been in school for over a year. He was running the streets for survival, without any home life. It took us two weeks to get the courts to see it our way and agree that he was in danger! The system denied us the status of emergency guardianship on a Friday. I told them, "Someone is either going to get hurt over the weekend – or even killed – if they don't listen to us!" Sure enough, the father of our nephew shot himself in the leg that weekend while hanging a gun on a nail. We found this out on Monday morning – and our Emergency Guardianship papers were handed to us in four hours!

Of course, legal papers were no match to a child on the streets. Once we found our nephew – and once his Auntie Jeannie showed him the papers, in love, from a thirty-foot distance – he ran! He took off over fences, and then who knows where. We went to the police, showed them our legal papers for his guardianship, and gave them a photo I'd taken of him two weeks earlier. I knew we would need it, but hoped that we wouldn't. An hour later, he was brought into the police station – and that became the moment of decision for our nephew. He got to make a choice: either come with us, or be charged with possessing certain items that were found on him. He was looking at going home with his aunt and uncle that night, to live with his three cousins, or going to juvenile hall. It was going to be his choice. The pivotal moment came from the six-foot-plus tall man sitting next to me – not just big, but also intimidating, as I recall. He was waiting to report his car stolen. He just couldn't take the drama of this boy acting all tough and not wanting to go with us – he might go, then he might not. This man said to our nephew, "Boy, if I'd had people like this wanting to give me a better life, I'd have done it! I didn't. And look at me, look closely – I've had a *rough* life! Take stock of what you have in front of you this moment – and choose well." Our nephew burst into tears, and then agreed to come with us. The officer told him, "It's just for a few weeks; then you can tell the judge what you want to do," so off we went! This was the beginning of our five-plus-year journey, and what a ride we went on! One last note on that night – our nephew looked hungry, so In-N-Out Burger was our first stop. We later learned that he was malnourished, and hadn't eaten in three days.

Much more went on during the coming weeks after our police station fiasco. I wanted you to see how our journey started, on the day we were called in to the hospital at his birth – and also, to know some of the hurt that he'd endured during the next fourteen years before we obtained guardianship. Our sideline journey was a long one, and in hindsight, I wish we had tried taking him in at a younger age. Hurting and watching the pain for years did none of us any good — all of us felt the hurt, and our nephew's life unfolded in an unsavory manner. In retrospect, Jeannie and I wish we had not been afraid to make waves in the family, and reached out to help him sooner. We did not engage in a guardianship proceeding until we got the call that something needed to be done for him.

One more thing: don't let guilt set in. Here's what I mean. You may not have jumped in to protect your guardian child as soon as you now think you should have. This can only poison your current situation. If you are now reflecting on the past, as we did many times, "If we'd only obtained guardianship sooner," you have to stop thinking this way! It won't help you at all, and furthermore, it will only inhibit you from being the best guardian you can be. Guilt never produces a positive outcome. You need to grab hold of it and toss it out the window as often as it pops its ugly head up. Guilt will only keep you from making good choices in your guardianship role. You're a guard now. Accept your new role – don't reflect on the shoulda-coulda-woulda. You're now raising the leaders of the future!

Chapter Recap

If you're contemplating a move on taking guardianship, count the cost of waiting. Move forward with boldness, stop the pain you may see, and know you are making a difference. You will endure a different pain, namely the pain of taking action. *This* pain, though, will "build your muscles" to protect the child more and more. Go after those who oppose you as peacefully as you can. Stop hurting from the sidelines! No one wins if you wait too long. Get in there – then show them what family does! In our case, we did what we could to provide a better life for our nephew's last five teenage years. Find your village to come alongside you to support your decision to make a difference!

Chapter Five

Think You're Too Young?

There is no standard "guardian profile." Guardians come in all ages and ethnicities, all shapes and sizes. It's very possible that the only relative available to step in and care for a child is a sibling or cousin who may still be quite young themselves. When this happens, as with any age, there is great sacrifice involved. This young guardian may already be married, but without their own children as yet. Some may have one or more small children of their own, and now, due to their new commitment, they can no longer give them the same amount of time and attention. When this happens, it is important to find a balance so that resentment does not set in. In Chapter Twenty-One I will discuss in more detail the subject of life being out of balance.

I know of some who took in a niece or nephew while single, which brought a new set of issues. The fact of not being able to date much due to the responsibility of raising a child could

It's very possible that the only relative available to step in and care for a child is a sibling or cousin who may still be quite young themselves. When this happens, as with any age, there is great sacrifice involved.

bring fear that they will never get the chance now to meet "Mr. (or Ms.) Right." I feel that by embracing the role of parenting a child in guardianship, they will be *more* likely, at the right time, to meet someone. This person will acknowledge and support their sacrifice by coming alongside them in the role of guardian. It won't be easy, and it may take years before this happens. If this is your situation, I encourage you to keep on keeping on. It will come back to you eventually, and it will be worth the wait. If you are a young guardian parent, you especially will need to find some good support people among your friends and family to assist you. This will be vital as you navigate your journey.

I would like to share with you the touching story of a young lady from England. She took on the challenge of raising her sister's children at a very early age. Her roller-coaster ride of emotions will touch your heart. This story is written in her own words:

My name is Emily, I'm twenty-three and I live in England. I have what we call over here a "Special Guardianship Order" for my sister's children; my nephew who is six and my niece who is five. This means that I am raising these children like my own until they are eighteen. I have overriding parental responsibility of the two children, though my sister still has some parental responsibility.

It all started back in 2010, just a few weeks after my niece was born. My sister had left the father of the children alone with my niece in her flat, while she took my nephew with her to the shop. She returned to see an ambulance outside. As she went upstairs, to her horror, she found out that they were there for her newborn daughter. She had suffered fractured ribs and a big gash just above her right eye that needed stitches.

Since that incident, the children were taken out of my sister's care by Social Services and placed temporarily with my dad and stepmother. Social Services had told my sister that she can have the children back in her care, but only if she doesn't go anywhere near their father again. The children went back to her, and everyone thought they were safe. But one night my brother went to their flat unexpectedly, and found that their abusive father was there again. My brother phoned the police, who came and removed the father. Social Services came in the middle of the night and took the children once again, this time putting them into foster care.

The children were in foster care for almost two years. Social Services had been assessing my sister while the children had contact with her three times a week. My sister put my name forward to have the children if

I was nineteen the day I found out that I would be going through assessments, parenting courses and classes to be able to get the children in my care.

— Emily, 19 year old guardian parent

she couldn't ever get the children back. Toward the end of the two years that the children were in foster care, Social Services deemed her "Not Suitable" to ever have the children back, and the case went to court.

The court day was horrible. We were all there as a family to support my sister, even though she had lied to us and put her children in danger. She was still my sister and I had to be there for her. The news came as a massive blow to her, and she broke down in the public bathroom crying. I remember hugging her and telling her, "Don't worry, I'll fight for them and I'll get them in my care." I was nineteen the day I found out that I would be going through assessments, parenting courses and classes to be able to get the children in my care. At this time I was even more panicked because I had serious self-esteem issues. I wasn't confident in myself, and I could barely talk to a stranger without almost having an anxiety attack. On April 10th, 2012, my assessments started. They took place every day for three weeks. I was watched while I did everyday activities with my nephew and niece – bathing them, changing diapers, playing with them, taking them outside, cooking for them and more. I was watched every second, and it was intense.

At the end of the assessments, I was told that I had passed. A few weeks later we were back in court, and I was awarded with a "Residency Order," meaning that the children could come and live with me while I was waiting to go back to court again for the "Special Guardianship Order." I was living with my dad and stepmother at the time, and in July, 2012, a day after my niece's second birthday, the children moved in. All the stress, all the heartache of missing them, and all the panic of the "what ifs?" was over. In September of 2012, I was awarded with the "Special Guardianship Order," meaning I now had parental responsibility. The next day my nephew started nursery school, and things were finally starting to feel normal again.

In November 2012, I got my own house, and in December, I moved out of my parents' home. At first I felt awkward, being the children's aunt, but making the mom decisions for them. My sister and I didn't really have a relationship. I had developed a lot of resentment towards her, and I was struggling to even talk to her the way we once used to. We would argue and fall out often, and I couldn't trust her to not lie to me again. I went through many stages of feeling alone, feeling as though there was no one like me in this world. I felt I was missing out on a normal life, and feeling sorry for the children I was raising.

Over the years since then, my relationship with my sister has finally come back on track, and she respects all of the choices that I make, and have made, for her kids. She

> *I went through many stages of feeling alone, feeling as though there was no one like me in this world. I felt I was missing out on a normal life, and feeling sorry for the children I was raising.*
> — Emily, 19 year old guardian parent

knows that I would do anything for them, and I know that she appreciates me. The resentment has faded, and she makes an effort with the children. The whole experience has changed me into a different person. I'm more outgoing, I'm more confident in myself, and I feel I've grown up really quickly to become who I am today. The children are thriving. They love their life. They have a bond with me which is indescribable, and they also have a great bond with their mother.

I've come to know more families who are also "kinship families," and the children have grown up to be positive about their situation. They're always happy to tell their friends that they don't live with a mommy or daddy, and that it's okay, because they live with an aunt who loves them just as much. They have awesome little friends who are so accepting of them and their life, and it's amazing to see them all grow up together. Kinship care has helped to keep these innocent children from growing up in the foster system, and it has allowed them to grow up with their family who love them so much. Everything I have done for them I would do again – over and over.

My wife and I have followed this young lady's journey for a few years now. One thing I would say is that you just can't get much younger than this to begin a journey of parenting in guardianship. As you can see, the growth curve was absolutely huge for her, and the emotional curve was painful. She carried on, and she has been rewarded in many ways. One thing I would like to add is that her brother Michael has been very involved too, and he shows the children a huge amount of love and support. He is very supportive in the way he has helped Emily along the way. He has played the role of her most active support person.

In their case, love and the desire to protect these children prevailed, as the bio-parents were not in any position to be parents to these children. I am convinced that if you or someone you know are contemplating a move toward guardianship to protect a child, you should be inspired to move on it quickly. Remember that the price you pay to protect the child will never add up to the price that the child will pay if you don't. Godspeed to you!

Chapter Recap

While being too young may be a concern you may have, I don't want to push anyone to do something that they don't feel would be a natural course for their life. Raising someone else's child is a huge undertaking. If you do so, please, please be sure to get a great group of support people around you. If it is meant to be, you will fall in love and never regret a moment of the time spent. This young lady did just that. Your choice should be one in which, once decided and in place, you would never turn back and change one moment. Or you could say it this way, "I would do it all over again."

Chapter Six

Regrets Be Gone

I want to take a few minutes here to address those who may have regrets. They come in various forms, so it is a bit complicated. First of all, how are we to predict the outcome of other people's poor choices? Would you say you feel or felt responsible in some way? Do you think you should have done more? The questions go on and on. And the truth is that while you were living your normal life, others were making poor choices, which one day came to affect you, and perhaps those around you as well. This is common with those who end up having their child taken from them. We must remember that during the years they were actively destroying their families, we were caring for our own in the best way we knew. Living with regrets for not doing

Taking the time to clear your mind of the past will produce better decision-making skills for the future.

enough is not a good mindset to be in. Now, I am not saying that a healthy bit of reflection wouldn't be helpful. The child in your care depends on your making good decisions or giving good advice. If you are a support person to a guardian, they need your help to move out of the zone of regret. Living in regret is not the place for brave warriors who are doing what someone else wouldn't or couldn't! You are doing very important work in life, and it's not right for you to feel any guilt for being the person standing in the gap for a child.

Taking the time to clear your mind of the past will produce better decision-making skills for the future. Someone once told me that there are two days in our lives that we cannot do anything about. My mind raced, trying to figure out which days those are. Along the way I started guessing, which only made things worse. What's the answer? The two days are yesterday and tomorrow! We must live in the present day and make the best possible choices. If we live too much in our yesterday, we will be clouded with regret — too much in our tomorrow and we will not focus on the tasks at hand that we need to accomplish now. Better decisions that we make today will affect our tomorrow in a positive way. Let's not regret that we didn't get guardianship sooner, or that the child wasn't in our care longer. Let's focus on what we can do for the child *today*. You are a special person because you care, and you want to see a good outcome for the child. So let's not get caught up in areas where we can't change the past, because this is unproductive.

We're hardly prepared for our own children – let alone the ones we are surprised with as guardians!

Case in point: I was visiting with a friend, who shared a bit about raising a niece in an informal arrangement. He first told me about the drama that led up to this, and how the whole family was affected. His family was the best choice at the time, because everyone had agreed that he and his wife had strong family values and were raising their children well. This is how they got elected. The hard part of their life was the limited budget they were on, due to working in the ministry. They had big hearts, but funds were very limited. This arrangement, he told me, had happened twelve years before this writing. Their niece lived with them for a year and a half. She began to thrive in their care, but the fact that it wasn't a formal arrangement created problems. The

Better decisions that we make today will affect our tomorrow in a positive way.

girl's mother started doing a bit better and wanted her daughter to come back. With the combination of tight finances and the informal arrangement my friend and his wife had regarding their niece, they had to comply. As my friend reflected on this, and watched his niece grow up, he was filled with regret. She took an unsavory direction in life, a very dark path. Over time, this began to correct itself, and she is doing better now. But he went through a time of regret, feeling that if she had stayed with them, her life could have been different. This is a heartbreaking position to be caught up in, and it caused a great deal of pain. Thankfully it is better now, and they have all survived the choices. My encouragement to him was "You did what you could with what you had," which is the best anyone could ask. We're hardly prepared for our own children – let alone the ones we are surprised with as guardians!

I am sure that one day guardians will be recognized for the billions of dollars they save taxpayers. It is my hope that funds could become available for guardian families, regardless of income status, to help offset the costs of caring for someone else's child, whether that person is a family member or not. I know it takes a lot of money to bring a child into your home. Grandparents feel this hit especially hard when guardianship enters their world.

Chapter Recap

Please take some time to clear your mind of any regrets you may be carrying. Take a run at the day one more time. Do what you can to make a difference here and now. I am confident that you will feel better. Everyone who touches the life of a child to make a difference is a special person. It will not only make the child feel better – but your own heart will mend in ways words cannot describe.

As you clear the slate of potential regrets, you may even see your energy level increase. Regrets can be debilitating, and this may keep you from having the strength to live up to your role as a guardian. Ask yourself if you can do something about that past issue, and if you can't, move on! If you can, resolve it! Regrets be gone!

Chapter Seven

You're the Best Choice

The best choice and the right choice always seem to intersect. You may have been led to read **Guardian Shift** because you feel inadequate. Well, the good news is that this makes you the best and the right person to be in charge! You're the guardian who guards, which makes you the top pick. Okay... enough on how *I* think of you – you need to begin to realize who *you* are in the greater scheme of things, the big picture. I know you're *the one!* Current events could be making you feel like the least likely candidate at this point. We are going to work on that. Just remember who everyone came to in their time of need. It was you! The decision was probably a hard one for you, too, and complicated by either not having your own children or having them. You're now a guardian because you have been making right choices in managing your life. Courts don't give this job to just anyone! I am sure your life has changed in many ways – because *you* stepped up.

The big-hearted person you are is what motivated you to take on this position. You certainly aren't doing it for the money! You opened your whole life up to help, risking the quality of life you already had. My guess is that some of your world remained the same and other areas changed. No matter at what age your guardian child came to you, it's a paradigm shift for everyone in your household. Having the openness to take in a hurting family member comes from a space deep in your soul. I hope that by this time you understand why *you* are the best choice to care for this child. You may be saying "I did it because no one else would," and that's okay too. We were called to take in our nephew because we already had three sons and it seemed to be a natural fit.

You're now a guardian because you have been making right choices in managing your life. Courts don't give this job to just anyone!

My wife and I were not equipped for the new family dynamics. We knew we were the right choice, though, because of the call on our hearts. It is big-hearted people like you, and like my wife and me, who will take in a child. I will get into the daily life later, but I need you to have a bit of a shift before I can do that. This shift is something like what you do in the case of an emergency on a plane. Nope, I'm not helping with flying lessons here… but if you have flown before, which many of us have in the age we live in, I would like you to recall the flight instructions. The flight attendant flips on the recording and does a little follow-along with her seat cushion and oxygen mask. If you haven't flown in a while, you may be a bit foggy on this. The attendant tells you (the adult) to put your own mask on first before the child's, right? Why? So you flipping don't pass out while you're trying to help the child. If you did, then you would *both* be in a world of hurt!

In this chapter, I tell you why caring for yourself is so very important. It goes like this: You must get your oxygen mask on first, meaning you must know the role you play in this flight / journey of guardianship. You must first, not in a prideful way, understand your role in saving this child's life. You're the key player who will struggle with this child so they can have a full life as an adult. If it weren't for you, this child would have gone down a very different path in life – possibly without hope or a chance. You are the most valuable player in this journey! So get your head where it needs to be. We are not going to make it until you embrace your role.

I struggled with my position a few too many times until my good friend Tim gave me a good verbal throttling. (Tim, by the way, was the guy who showed up in court and supported us as we were getting guardianship of our nephew, driving 100 miles each way, too!) He was one of our closest support people, and he saw our drive and desire to protect our nephew. I told him we were just doing our part. He insisted we were more than that. I have to say it was hard to receive his kind words, but they eventually sank in. I remember Tim saying, on several occasions, "The changes I see in your nephew are a direct result of what a good job you are doing." Well, I never saw it like that, except for a few times. Tim went on further to tell me, "One day you must write a book about this." I was like, "Are you nuts? I / we are barely making it through the guardianship role we are in, let alone writing a book on the subject." This is what I get for doubting the love of a true friend like Tim. We all need

The importance of accepting that you're the best choice for this new role is key to your successful journey.

one in our lives! What a good man! For fifteen years I have had the freedom to vent on and be encouraged by him, and I value our friendship very highly.

Putting all the drama you deal with aside, I now crown you the BEST PERSON for the job! I am going to assume that you fully understand the gravity of taking care of yourself first. You are the life support to the child in your care. I am confident we can move on to working on problems that are everyday occurrences, which you as a guardian are facing. You have your game on now – you know the role you play! Now that you can see it my way, you can get your head into the rest of this book. Together we are going take a crack at putting your life back in control of the oxygen. Once your child learns the role you play and the role they are in, you both will have a better flight…!

Chapter Recap

The importance of accepting that you're the best choice for this new role is key to your successful journey. Hold onto the fact that you are in the right place at the right time. It's no mistake. Remember to take care of yourself so that you can maintain your energy and your mental well-being. You may never get the validation you need or deserve – but just know you that are the right person. Those around you know you are! Each and every day, write down one or more positive occurrences to reflect on. By doing this simple act daily, you will begin to feel empowered – and that's like putting on your own oxygen mask!

Chapter Eight

Grandparent Glue

Grandparents are the glue when the vase shatters. They have lived many years, and over the years they have gained a great deal of wisdom. While doing some research, I came across an article in *USA Today,* written by Cheryl Makin.[1] Below is a quote from it. The numbers have continued to grow.

"According to 2010 U.S. Census data, 4.9 million American children are being raised solely by their grandparents. The number is almost double that of the 2000 Census – 2.4 million."

I have a ton of respect for all of you grandparents who have taken in a grandchild or grandchildren. Many of you do it at an age when you should not have to be dealing with raising children. You're at the stage in life when grandparents play with them, enjoy their time with them, and then send them

There is a possibility that you are raising the next president, the next Oprah, or the founder of some sort of technology that will help change lives of people all over the world.

home to their parents at the end of the day or weekend. Sadly enough, though, you are now serving as a parent to your grandchild as well as your child. This is mentally, physically and financially draining, but you have done it out of love. You know that if you don't take your grandchildren in, who will? You didn't want to see them end up in the foster care system. You did what you have done for years: namely, pull your bootstraps up and dig into being a parent once again.

Grandparents have been responsible for many successful people in this world. They have raised some of our world leaders, American presidents, musicians, actors – the list goes on and on. You can search the subject online and see just who they are. I won't take any time here to cite them all, though I do encourage you to do this research. They're easy to find, and some of the stories are really much like yours and mine – more common than one might think. The best part of each of the stories I have read is how these well-known people give tribute to their grandparents for laying the foundation for their lives. Some of them state that if it hadn't been for their grandma or grandpa, they would not have known the value of hard work. Grandparents have lived life long enough to know that anything is possible. Some of these famous people are in their sixties and above, and their grandparents got to live through times that were pretty harsh. They knew the value of a hard day's work, and how it could lead not only to survival, but to life-changing success! There is a possibility that you are raising the next president, the next Oprah, or the founder of some sort of technology that will help change lives of people all over the world. The most important fact, though, is that you are tending to the well-being of a child. This is your calling, and it is to be respected. One day your child will show their appreciation for the sacrifices you made to raise them. Just be patient.

In 2006, while living in Puerto Vallarta, we made a very dear friend, Sudy Coy. My dear Sudy is the sweetest lady, and she is always connecting people together. When we met her, she was serving so many children through one of the local orphanages that it made my head spin. Fast forwarding to the end of 2015, she is still an advocate for orphans and the well-being of the Puerto Vallarta community. She recently connected me with a friend of hers, Dave Tomlin, for which I am so very grateful. Dave's life, and his wife's (during their retirement years) have been forever changed. He shares his story with us:

> *It's January in the mountains, and I'm feeling a little sorry for myself these days as I shovel snow from the front walk and scrape the ice from the windshield of my pickup truck.*

> *God forbid that the snowpack on the road should get slick enough to force me to install the chains I just bought for my knobby, oversized tires. I've never mounted chains before, but I'm told there are times that my four-wheel drive may not be enough to get us up the*

steep, winding hill to our front door after a big storm.

This is not the way Pam and I had planned to spend our winter months in retirement. On the contrary, we planned very carefully to do exactly the opposite.

More than a decade ago, when we were both still working in New York City, we bought a three-bedroom condo in Puerto Vallarta on the Pacific coast of Mexico with the idea that it would be our primary residence when we were ready to hang it up.

We had also inherited, from Pam's dad, a small lot with big mountain views in Ruidoso, New Mexico. We figured we could build a cabin there and use it as a spring/summer retreat from the tropical heat. In our dream scheme, we'd spend about half the year in each place, following 80-degree days and 60-degree nights up and down the continent on a timetable enforced only by our whim and the weather. Then something happened that changed everything. We suddenly became parents again.

Pam's adult daughter Heather, from her first marriage, gave premature birth nearly six years ago in Albuquerque to a daughter, Elizabeth. The baby weighed less than three pounds and went immediately into neonatal intensive care. Heather was discharged a few days later, but was returned by police to the hospital almost immediately after symptoms of her bipolar disorder returned.

She was still there several weeks later when the hospital called us in New York to advise us that Elizabeth was ready to leave the hospital and that she would be released to foster care if no family member showed up to take custody.

We should have seen this moment coming. I helped raise Heather from the time she was a toddler. We both experienced the onset of her mental illness after her first year of college, and watched it lay waste to her entire adult life. She was hospitalized repeatedly for psychotic breaks and suicide attempts, and in addition to dozens of brief committals she spent months in locked wards where we hoped specialized treatment would somehow restore her to health.

Her pregnancy was a bad idea, to put it mildly, and of course we did our best to discourage it. By the time it happened, however, she was past forty years old and far beyond our influence.

At first, things seemed to go okay. Heather spent the last few months of her term in a hospital bed due to medical complications, and in that stress-free ambience of total care her symptoms took a holiday. She seemed almost like her old self, and very excited to be an expectant mother.

Elizabeth's father, Zack, had disappeared from the scene months earlier. But we told ourselves that with her Social Security disability benefits, supported housing and an attentive case worker, Heather might be able to pull it off. Even after she got sick again after giving birth, we tried to believe that there was time while the baby was in neonatal care for Heather to get her symptoms back under control.

When the hospital called, we were forced to stop kidding ourselves and do the soul-searching overnight that we should have been doing all along. The next day we got on a plane for Albuquerque to collect Elizabeth. She was the tiniest baby either of us had ever held, still a bit less than five pounds and urgently in need of careful monitoring, special nutrition and as much weight gain as we could give her.

Even then, as we flew back to New York, we clung to the hope that our custody would be temporary. We installed a crib in the dining area of our 550-square-foot Manhattan apartment and began the endless cycle of high-fat feedings that Elizabeth needed. Pam organized a rotation of close friends who could each give us a weekly half-day of relief so we could attend to the lives and careers we were pursuing before all this happened.

And when Heather was discharged from the hospital, we brought her to New York and got her into a women's shelter as the first step toward gaining a spot in a halfway house that specialized in the chronically and severely mentally ill.

But it soon became clear that for the foreseeable future, motherhood for her was out of the question. Her visits with Elizabeth caused emotional stress for all of us and probably aggravated her symptoms. She blamed us for taking her child and soon began accusing us of abusing Elizabeth. On one traumatic occasion she called the police, who rushed to our apartment with medical personnel to investigate. We were forced to accompany them to a nearby emergency room where pediatricians conducted an invasive examination.

We had obtained guardianship status in order to qualify Elizabeth for coverage under my company health insurance. The police incident made us realize that for the sake of Liz's future security and stability, we needed to move immediately to terminate Heather's parental rights, brutal as it sounded, and adopt Elizabeth. Only then would we have undisputed rights to keep her with us and make all decisions about her care and future.

Not long after Liz's second birthday, we finally got our court order and she was truly ours. Remembering the moment when the judge pronounced us mom and dad still brings tears to my eyes and a lump to my throat.

By that time, we were no longer living in New York. We'd decided to try going ahead with our original retirement plans, and it seemed to work pretty well. Each fall we went to Mexico. We enrolled Elizabeth in a private Mexican preschool, where she quickly picked up Spanish from her teachers and playmates. We did our best to keep up, with conversation classes of our own.

We even did a little of the traveling in Mexico that we had dreamed of. The highlight was a trip to the mountains of Michoacan to see the giant clusters of monarch butterflies that drape the pine trees of their winter nesting grounds. Liz said she was scared of horses when she saw that getting to the butterflies would require a trail ride. But when the guide lifted her up to sit in front of me, she said after a few minutes that she liked OUR horse. A few hours later, on the way back to the parking lot, she fell asleep in the saddle.

We decided we liked being parents in Mexico better than we would have liked being just another pair of retired gringos. We gladly gave up the happy hour carousing, beach bumming and bridge classes that might have become our expatriate lifestyle. Instead, we socialized with the close circle of young families at Liz's school. We helped Liz with her homework and took her to swimming classes and birthday parties. It struck us as a richer and more natural routine than the one we had imagined.

> *We're already in our late sixties. Our health is still good, but the odds of that continuing to be true for both of us grow a bit longer with each passing year.*
> – *Dave Tomlin, Grandparent*

Each April or May, when the weather began getting warm, we made the drive north to Ruidoso. Liz went to another preschool for half days. But whenever we felt like it, we pulled her out and took off for tours of national parks with our little Airstream trailer.

We also made an annual late-spring or early-summer trip to New York to visit our other adult daughter who teaches school there, and to take Elizabeth to see her mother, who by then had been committed for long-term treatment at a state psychiatric hospital. Until we left New York, we had taken Elizabeth to see Heather every few weeks. When we moved to Mexico, we had a phone call every Sunday, except during times when her mother's condition made that impossible.

Elizabeth chose on her own almost as soon as she could speak to call us Mommy and Daddy, but she has understood all her life who her biological mother is and that she's with us because Heather was unable to take care of her.

Her father Zack had met Heather when they were both patients at a hospital in New York. Zack was diagnosed with schizophrenia. We didn't know where he was when Elizabeth was born. But he got in touch with us when Elizabeth was four, and asked for pictures and maybe a chance to see her. We said we might arrange it if we could speak first with his principal case worker. On our visit to New York last summer, the two of them met for the first time in Central Park. It went beautifully. She embraced the stuffed animals he brought her and then hugged him without being invited to, much as she does with our close friends.

At age five, Elizabeth doesn't seem to think or talk much at all about her natural parents. In their presence or by phone, she's polite but loses interest quickly. Yet we know her curiosity about them will grow as she gets older. Our hope is that she'll get to know them better in *her own time and at her own pace without any sense from us that she's venturing into sensitive territory.*

Heather is out of the hospital now, has married another fellow patient, and unfortunately has given birth again. This time she remained healthy after the baby arrived and six months later was still caring for him, though with difficulty. We often wonder what Elizabeth thinks or feels about the fact that Heather is caring for another child after failing to care for her. But we have other concerns that seem far more serious to us.

As the offspring of two parents with psychiatric disorders, Elizabeth's genetic heritage may contain the seeds of future vulnerability to illness of her own. We don't want, by thought, word or deed, to make this a self-fulfilling prophecy. But as Elizabeth approaches her pre-teen years, we will be on the alert in spite of ourselves for signs that we all may need professional help.

By that time, our own capacity for dealing with trouble – if it comes – will be diminished. We're already in our late sixties. Our health is still good, but the odds of that continuing to be true for both of us grow a bit longer with each passing year. Last year as we were starting to plan for Liz's first year in "real" school, we began asking ourselves if it was smart to go forward with our plan to put her in one of the very good private primary-secondary schools in Vallarta.

If health concerns, or anything else, prompted us to move back to the U.S. several years down the road, wouldn't the transition from private Mexican to U.S. public school be a harsh one for our daughter?

For that reason, we decided last spring, shortly after returning to Ruidoso for the summer, to look into the public kindergarten program here. We were pleasantly surprised at what we found. Out of the local school district's eight kindergarten classes, two are dual-language. While designed mainly for kids from Spanish-speaking homes, there's room in them for a limited number of English-speaking kids.

The mix is good for all of them. The Spanish speakers get an immediate taste of studying side by side with the English-speaking mainstream school population. The English speakers learn some Spanish and, hopefully, the value of diversity. And after the dual-language learning runs its five-year course, studies show that all the participants, going forward, perform better academically than the student body at large.

So last fall we enrolled Liz in the Ruidoso school system, where I'm happy to report that she appears to be thriving. That is a great relief to us. We love her very dearly and are wholly devoted to her well-being. Had it not turned out well, this decision would have been very hard to undo, although I still figure we've got about a year in which we could do it if we had to.

As it did in Mexico, being parents in Ruidoso seems to have drawn us more thoroughly into the life of the community than we would have been without Elizabeth.

I offered to cover local schools for the twice-weekly newspaper as a freelancer, and ended up with a full-time reporting job. Pam has immersed herself in local non-profit work and is looking for a way to exercise the mental-health counseling skills she acquired with her master's degree in the years just before we left New York. We both feel much busier and more productive than we might have pushed ourselves to be if Elizabeth's presence in our lives hadn't energized us. And all of that comes on top of the main prize – her ever-emerging personality and our growth together as a trio. Nearly six years in, I don't think any one of us can now imagine life without the other two.

For the joy this new nuclear family has brought me, I would shovel snow to Mexico and back if that's what it takes to keep it.

As I said before Dave's story, I am grateful for him and his wife. They not only had careers that demanded their time, but the years of planning their retirement were now changed forevermore. The love they have for their adopted granddaughter is so apparent. The sacrifice they made has turned into doing them a favor. This shift they found themselves in has created a vitality they would not have known if they had not said yes to taking in their granddaughter.

Chapter Recap

Grandparents are super glue in my opinion! The wisdom they possess from their years of life is hard to match, however you look at it. If it weren't for grandparents, society as a whole would be in a world of hurt. If you know someone who is caring for their grandchildren, find a way to help them out a bit – this will recharge their batteries. They are so strong in their minds, but as we know, in many cases the will is sometimes more powerful than the body. We all need a break from time to time.

Chapter Nine

Wow! A Handful

As I mentioned before, when we became guardians, we only knew of one other family who were guardians also. Their grandson was in our oldest son's Awana group, and the boys were friends. We had known the Browns for a few years. They'd had guardianship of their grandson since he was six years old, and he is now twenty-seven. Let me tell you, he was a handful. My dear friend and his wife loved it when they could just get a little break. Remember, they were to be enjoying their "Golden Years," not running to PTA meetings! Yet this is what they were doing, and so much more! Their little guy was full of energy, and since we were quite a bit younger than they were, we loaded their grandson up into our car, and brought him home with us, many times. We had four boys in the house at the time, so it was already a free-for-all at our place – skateboarding, building ramps, swimming at the neighbor's house, and then off to see movies. They were gracious to us whenever we needed to drop one or two of ours off, and they did their best to keep up with them.

It is great how Dave Tomlin and his wife have felt more productive and energized while raising their young granddaughter. I am sure it has had the same effect for many guardian grandparents. But not all. Many I have spoken with feel exhausted, both physically and emotionally. It can be taxing for anyone to take on the task of raising a grandchild during this time in their life. I have a big soft spot in my heart for you! For those of you reading this, whether you are or aren't a guardian, I encourage you to find a way to arrange for support to get a break for yourself (if you are the guardian) or to give a break (if you are not a guardian, but a "Support Team" member). More often than not, someone would love to step up and help – they just need to know that help is needed. This my biggest reason for wanting to write this book – to build awareness and to bring people together, helping one another. Grandparents can experience health issues, and opportunities for taking a break in their new roles as guardians are few and far between. Helping them get involved in networks with other guardians is a great way for them to find some relief.

I just met a lady at a function that my wife and I were attending. After a brief conversation, she asked me what kind of work I do. I told her I was in the midst of writing a book series on parenting children in guardianship. "What do you mean?" she asked. I answered, "You know, when an aunt, uncle or grandparent steps in and raises you." She said, "That's me and my siblings – this is how we were raised. I had no clue what it was called. My parents both died when I was very young." Now,

I must tell you that this conversation is taking place in Puerto Vallarta, Mexico, where they don't have a foster care system. If you have no one to take you in, you go to the orphanage. With that said, after her parents died, family members dropped her and her siblings off with an aunt and uncle. In a short period of time, the aunt and uncle took everything the children had – it was awful. When their grandma (age 73) heard about this, she was furious, and took all three children in by herself. Grandma had very little, but what she *did* have was the ability to make ends meet and care for them. This was a hardship on her, as the children were only eleven, fourteen and sixteen at the time. The sixteen-year-old went to work to help bring money in, and then the others followed suit over time. It's impressive to me that her grandma never made it seem as though things were tight; the children understood it much later in life. Grandma lived until she was 99 years old, and she gave these three youngsters a path in life that no one else was ever going to give them.

Many of you are living on a fixed income. I realize that some seem to be losing ground on making ends meet. If Social Security is your main source of income, it could be falling short of meeting your monthly expenses. Each state is a bit different on providing resources to those of you in this position. It is not my intention to know what your rights are, or what is available to you. However, I would like to share with you a website that is full of information according to state. When you get a chance, look at AARP's website and search for the "Grandfacts."[1] You can put in your state to find local resources.

I encourage you to seek some help if you need it. Don't be embarrassed; it is not your fault you are parenting again. No one has ever begrudged paying taxes that would help families with a real need. Make a few phone calls, or have someone else do it for you. I am confident that you can find someone who would love to help you.

Many of you have shared in conversation with me that schooling and homework can be daunting. It is a different world at this stage in life. I have no clue, at age fifty-five, what all of this "common core" math is about. The school system I am familiar with used to focus on math, English, writing, science and of course my favorite, the agriculture department, since I was a farmer's son. I personally don't understand how so many of you do it. I was fortunate that our nephew had our sons to ask for help with schoolwork, as well as his friends, with subjects where my knowledge was outdated. Now, I do understand that using extreme math is how we put a man on the moon, so I have a great deal of respect for math and why we must be proficient in it.

A tutor sounds like the only logical thing to me if there are no other options. I think if you can find a suitable mentor who can help your child with school, this is how I would handle it now. A word of caution: I recommend that the tutor you choose would have come to you with solid references that you can verify. I am not endorsing any one method – just make sure you know who your child is being tutored by, and where. You want to know that the values you are trying to instill in your child are not being undermined.

I know that some of you may be a bit concerned with how you may feel when you show up at school. For example, in the area of events or conferences for your grandchildren, let me share my perspective personally. Jeannie and I raised our three sons and our nephew. Our youngest son was twelve years old when we were blessed to find out we were going to have another child. Yes, we were about to start all over again! It was such a blessing when little Gracie came into our lives in our forties. So with some gray in my beard, a little hair loss… we heard, "Oh, how old is your granddaughter?" more than I care to admit. So needless to say, I shaved most of the facial hair off and cut my hair shorter. Trust me, there is no fountain of youth, but it did cause us both to find ways to slow down the aging process a bit. The tough part was going to the kindergarten class to discover that most of those parents could be our children. Yikes! We worked through the innuendos of being thought of as the grandparents, and soon people came to a solid knowledge that we were the parents. It was making me a little self-conscious – and it has caused me to be especially sensitive to your position.

What can we do to minimize these difficulties for you? Some of you have already moved on to the fact that it's no big deal; others may be smack-dab in the middle of it now. The first thing we are going to do is learn who we are, as I spoke of earlier – so lift your head high and remember how important you are. You are saving a life, standing in the gap, making a difference in the future and security of a child. This is a big deal – remember it. The fact that you are older makes you stronger, bolder and much wiser. You have a heart of compassion – and a wealth of knowledge and experience – which goes a long way. Just think how much you know versus your younger counterparts at the school functions. Yes, times have changed, but wisdom just can't be bought – it's only earned and learned over time.

The biggest thing for you to do is to make sure your child understands how much you love them. This transcends all the gaps.

The next critical matter after you get through this age gap concerns the child in your care. In the beginning, kids don't realize that you are older until, well, some bully points it out to them. This is when your child becomes self-conscious about the age gap. Oh boy, this is the tough one. They understand that you are their protector, but they are conflicted with the fact that they are struggling with acceptance from their peers. Lots of changes have transpired for you both, and this is not easy. Do I have all the answers? Nope. But I know that once we have thousands of you linked up on a platform to encourage one another, we will find even more solutions to this issue. The biggest thing for you to do is to make sure your child understands how much you love them. This transcends all the gaps. Love is the biggest motivator, and it has to be unfailing – even in the tough times when it may be hard to love them.

School Relationships

After love comes good communication with your child – but you are going to need allies. Some of the most important allies spend many hours every day with your child. They are called teachers. Set up a private meeting with your child's teacher to explain your family dynamics. By the way, this is good for all of you aunties and uncles too! Help your child's teachers understand your family's situation. They will become your cheerleaders and advocates as time goes on. Please, please don't make them an enemy, which is easy to do if you are on the warpath toward righting a wrong done to your child. Let's assume you still have the opportunity to make a good connection with your child's teacher. They have training in the area of behavioral issues that could arise. They see the child in a different environment than we do, interacting with their peers while they attend classes. Let them give you their insights; tell them they are your eyes and ears and that you want to team up with them. Believe me, a teacher can make a great support person to you, helping you with challenges before they get out of hand.

I was raised on a farm, so who do you think in high school was my biggest advocate on the teaching staff? Yes, you guessed it, the agricultural teacher. When I was sixteen years old. my father had a triple bypass surgery. His farming operation consisted also of doing custom farm work for other farmers during the summer and fall seasons. They were all focused around harvesting almond and walnut crops. The issue arose, when he was unable to work, of who would cover one of the divisions of his company. Because I'd become acquainted with it over the years, I became the logical choice. The work I was to take on was the "orchard shaking," which shakes the nuts to the ground for harvest. My older brother, being quite talented, had trained me on much of the needed duties and stayed in close communication with me. Here's the problem: All of this happened at the beginning of my senior year, when school was starting back up. I only attended two weeks of the first quarter, and then left to run this part of my father's company on a full-time basis. Because this extended to the first week of November, I missed a total of nine weeks of school. In 1978, the schools were very open to working with children from farms, but I had kind of pushed the limits. Guess who came to the rescue? Mr. Bill Walker, my agriculture teacher, a stern yet caring man who understood life. He was able to get the school district to allow me a break, due to the family hardship. We always stayed in close communication with Mr. Walker and the school district. I was elated, and I would not have to carry the missed assignments over the balance of the school year.

I know firsthand how much a good relationship with your child's teacher can pay off. They want to help, and with the epidemic of displaced children in the USA, I know you will find an ear. As you navigate the balancing act of the generation gap of your child's having grandparents as parents, just know that most teachers are on your side. Some of you may already have this issue in check, and that is great! I encourage you to jump into our Guardian Shift Facebook group, where you can share your success stories with other guardians.

Time For A Break

As grandparents, you have worked a lifetime to retire and enjoy yourselves. Now you're at a time in your life that puts you back in the days of parenting and working around a school-year schedule. This can be restricting, and it can become a source of potential resentment. Not all of you will feel this way, but more than a few I have spoken to have. It's okay to feel this way, to some extent – I think it's only natural. Let's explore options for having a bit of freedom back in your life. Some of you may have a close friend who can come to live in your home so you can take those short trips to the sea or mountains. Some of you may need to find another guardian in your local area who can handle the extra responsibility of having another child in their home so that you can get away. However it comes together, let's not let you lose the splendor of traveling, if it is important to you.

Imagine with me, for a minute – what if you knew other guardians who might be in your local area who could help you out so you could get away? This is one of my goals: to have local groups in each city that could meet up together. This can change the dynamics for so many of us who may be contemplating taking in a child under guardianship. Soon, we will have small-group books that all guardians can use to facilitate group meetings. First, though, we have to get the word out about guardianship, and how it is such an overlooked form of parenting. While addressing the everyday life of this wild journey of parenting children in guardianship, we do want as much family balance as possible. At the same time, we will also build awareness, encouragement, healing – and plans for networking guardian families together.

Chapter Recap

Reflecting on this chapter, I realize I could have continued to expand it into a full book. It is hard enough to parent in today's world, and even harder to complicate things by raising a second generation. My hat is off to all of you! You possess wisdom from your years of life, and this makes you such wonderful caregivers for these children. I just wish I could give you a shot of youthfulness so that you'd have as much energy as those in your care. You are a powerful force, no matter what age you are – and we can learn so much from you! Please take care of all areas of your life, and network with others to find trustworthy people to come alongside you. Allowing others to help you will let *them* feel rewarded in helping *you* make a difference.

Chapter Ten

Reducing the Drama

How are you at separating the drama and keeping it out of the child's presence? The drama of hurt feelings is for "behind closed doors" only – and not near the child. They have been through enough. This may be hard if the child is older, because you may feel that since they were dealing with drama already, that they can handle hearing it. But this isn't necessarily true. I would suggest you try to minimize the drama they are exposed to, if at all possible.

If the children in guardianship are old enough to remember their mom and dad, they typically feel a strong bond of love for their parents. Even if the relationship is smeared with problems and abuse, this love bond is strong. A word of caution as you speak about the child's mom and dad. If you speak negatively about their parents to them, the child will go into protection mode on behalf of their parents. This will basically paralyze

Needless to say, the power of a hug, wrapped in an overtone of genuine love, is felt by the heart!

your new beginning with the child, and you will never get past first base. As much as you may want to vent and tell them of the wrongs, don't do it. It is hard, however, when you just went through a battle and have hurts all over the place. You're still making huge decisions too – like visitation, who wronged you in court, or who is still just a thorn in your side. In guardianship cases you're typically taking children from your own children, your brother, your sister or a close family friend. This is a touchy subject, and you may feel justified because of how your guardian child was treated. You may have been roughed up by other family members too. But don't bring any of it up. Connect with a good counselor, and get advice on how to resolve these hurts.

Let's get back on track with using love as our best ally. Love shows up in many forms, from sharing a cookie and a smile to giving the child a place to call home – but hugs are the universal language of love. Let me tell you about a young boy who had just turned fourteen and thought he needed to make a change in his life. For whatever reason, he felt it was time to run away and start his life elsewhere. Obviously, something was wrong at home. I am only going to touch on a few things to make my point. He was able to reroute his plan for running away to simply escaping to a friend's home for the weekend. The first night there, he noticed that all the children in the home hugged their parents before heading off to bed. This turned out to be awkward for this fourteen-year-old, as he had not been hugged by his mother since he was ten years old. The weekend grew into several months, as the family of the fourteen-year-old allowed their son to remain with the friend's family while they sorted matters out. With this young fellow, hugs started to become more natural, and they became a frequent way for him to greet others.

Smiles began to surface on this young man's face, which gave him a whole new look. He was almost unrecognizable, I am told, by those who hadn't seen him in a while. Needless to say, the power of a hug, wrapped in an overtone of genuine love, is felt by the heart! Using hugs with love is a powerful tool – and I can say that it is the fire that melts hurts and bonds hearts, creating trust. Without one word *spoken* of love, you can *show* love to your child with a simple hug. Of course, I would recommend caution when hugging a child who might view this loving act as an invasion of his or her personal space. Past issues could distort the child's view and bring up painful memories. Proceed with caution, as even the most loving and caring person could be misunderstood. Be aware of this as you enter into the delicate area where emotional wounds may still exist.

Some of you will uncover issues in your guardian child's past that you will be furious about. You will have to return to the foundation you have laid with your child. Eventually they will come to you for guidance, asking you for help to resolve a deep-seated conflict. They won't really care how much you are helping them until they know how much they can trust you. Kids need to feel loved – and sometimes a hug is better than mere words.

The foundation of trust and love that you have created will get your whole family through the times ahead. The honeymoon will end and the drama will begin – this is just life. The bond you have created needs to be protected, as much as you wish, to protect the child. If you're like me, you want to right every wrong that comes up. But this is just not a good plan. Your child doesn't need you to fix the past, as much as they need you to just help them walk through to the other side of it. They need you to remain calm, and not tear mom or dad apart. Always keep in mind the love the child has, no matter how bad things used to be with mom and dad. Your respect for their feelings will keep your child open to you – but the moment you cross that line, things change. Your heart is breaking as the new information about the real inner workings of their old life comes to light, and this raises your protection meter to red alert. I feel for you, but your child is hurting too! We walked this fine line ourselves, and we blew it on several occasions; we had one thing on our minds, and that was to right every wrong. After a few sessions with our counselor, though, we learned to calm down when new things were coming to light. It was at that point when things started to come to the surface more and more easily.

In some ways, you, the guardian, are wounded too. You have made a grandstand play to protect this child, and you have some pent-up hurts of your own. Reflecting on our guardianship, we had several people who were just plain angry with us for taking in our nephew, which is completely confusing to me. The family members who initially had called on us to do something then became our worst nightmare. Maybe you can relate? I hope this wasn't the case for you, but it may be. When you find yourself surrounded by family members who are less than supportive, it may be hard for you to keep your cool around the house. Everybody feels it, and its extended effects do permeate the children and the whole household. You are only human, and it is sometimes difficult to remain calm. But try your hardest to keep yourself from blowing up or, should I say, keep yourself from having a nuclear reaction!

You're hurt because you were the only one who cared enough to seek protection for the child, which is a concept that the others may or may not ever understand. You have to know that in some ways, they could feel jealous that you are now in a leadership role with the other person's child. You are now the go-to person for the bio-parents to get permission to see their child, which some bio-parents don't like. The hurt you feel is real, and it does need to be addressed. I touched on them earlier in the book, but we could use a refresher, as I am dredging up some dirt now. Remember who you are. It's best said like this: "Guardians *Guard*" – that's it! You are now the boss. So they will have to get over it and buckle up, because there is a "new sheriff in town." It will take a while for them to understand and accept the new role you play.

Just because the court says you are now the guardian over the life and estate of the child, it doesn't mean you are filling those boots all the way yet. So grab your bootstraps one more time, and saddle up! You are the guard, and that means that you make the decisions now. Let's think about it – why did the child end up in your care to begin with? It happened most likely because the bio-parents made some

Your child doesn't need you to fix the past, as much as they need you to just help them walk through to the other side of it.

poor choices that affected their child's life. Now they no longer make the decisions. You do. The fact that they are the birth parents doesn't gives them the right to try to boss you around. Okay, lets tone it down a bit. You just need to remember your position, and fill it with the facts. In no way am I saying to lord it over anyone. What I am saying is that if you want the respect of your guardian child, you need to be able to protect them in a loving manner.

Once again, a support person is a lifesaver. The brilliance of a good accountability partner will help you stay on course. Take your hurts to them, give them the full vent and let them know you don't want to dump this garbage anywhere near your family or home. This stuff is radioactive, and it will disrupt the balance in your home. I am sure that after a few "dumpings," you will feel better. Then you will not allow your hurts to well up, and overshadow your new calm-and-collected way of dealing with the troublemakers.

Attempt to be fair in your dealings with those who are unreasonable. Share, with a firm tone, a message along these lines: "This is how we do it now. You had your chance – and now it's mine to decide." After a few rounds of reminding them, they will eventually see the picture. Maintaining boundaries allows balance to come back in to your home and your life. There's no other way in which this can this be established. Once they see a few times how the new rules work, life will smooth out. You are the gatekeeper – and that is just the way it is. Over time, they will come to understand that this actually is good. It appears rough at first, but balance will come. The good work you are doing for the child is the most important factor to consider. Moreover, the only one who needs to respect you for the protection you provide is the child in your care!

Chapter Recap

All of us have unique stories of how our guardianship began. I am confident that most of us had drama to deal with. How we extinguish it is the hard answer to come up with. Separating out your emotions — who stepped on you, who lied to you... the list goes on – is the key. As we peer into our souls, one common bond comes to the surface in everyone's heart – our commitment to protect the child in our care. Displays of love develop over time, creating trust and unity. This will give both you and the child an open door to begin healing. Taking charge, as you have now been appointed to do, is not always easy – and as you do, the more and more natural it will become. Stand tall, know your role and become the guardian who guards!

Section Two

Adjusting to the Shift

Here in Section Two, "Adjusting to the Shift," I cover many areas to assist you in your changing world. When we add to the number in our existing family, we go through huge shifts. I'll be sharing insights from a young woman who, with her husband, stepped up and took in their two nieces and a nephew. They learned how to cope with going from no children to a family of five. I will give tips on handling those "bios" (biological parents) who want to claim the spotlight on special days. I'll address the tough calls on handling social media as a guardian. In addition to all of the above, I'll deal with a few tougher subjects that will show love to your child in guardianship, including ways to pull together a team to help you as you navigate. I will also address a few topics regarding teens in guardianship.

Adjusting to the shift in your life hits you at many different points of your guardianship, and I hope these topics will help to smooth out some challenges along the way for you.

Chapter Eleven

Your New Family Unit

You have done an amazing job of getting your guardian child protected, and into a loving environment. This, indeed, is the highest milestone of your guardianship journey, but the challenges of developing your new family unit are still in front of you. I am sure many of you have experienced some great successes in this area, but I have a few thoughts for you.

For my wife and me, we integrated one more teenage boy, who was nearly the same age as our oldest son at the time. You'd think this might be fairly easy, right? Well, sometimes it feels as if you're refereeing toddlers. Let's set up the scene this way. Imagine two preschoolers on the floor playing with toys. They are having a wonderful time at first, with lots of cute looks and grabbing the cars or dolls, until... you guessed it. They both want the same toy at the same exact time. That's when the war games begin. Tug and pull. Then the groans and screams start. This is the moment when you have to step in and break up the battle, and set the record straight on how the next few choices are to be made – or else! You may have gotten them straightened out for a moment, but you will have to jump back in the middle again soon. This, in my opinion, is the new dynamics of your emerging family, and, I might add, with children of any age. You may feel like a referee. Things get messy quickly, and a moment of fun can turn into exasperating parenting!

The child you brought into your home will probably need a lot of attention from you and/or your spouse, perhaps more than you expected. This can start an imbalance. At first your heart feels that it's the right thing, and you are correct in your judgment, but then, gradually, you start feeling overwhelmed. Guardians not only guard, they give of themselves unselfishly — body, soul, time and finances. Your friends and family simply cannot see your sacrifice until they have walked in your shoes. In doing so, we tend to lose ourselves in the quest of helping.

Guardians not only guard, they give of themselves unselfishly – body, soul, time and finances.

Let's start with those of you who don't have children. Either you have not yet had your own, hadn't planned to have any (or hadn't been able to), or have already raised your own and have become an empty nester. You have been in the just-you-and-me-babe stage of life. Everything is bliss. You make choices at the last minute to run out and see a movie, or stay up late having a nice dinner by candlelight. What your life consists of when it's just the two of you is much different from what it becomes when children come into the picture. As a couple without children, you have freedom of choice – and it is a great sacrifice when you give that up to take a child in under guardianship care.

You have been led to take on the responsibility of protecting this little one (or big one, if he or she is already a teenager). You begin to realize that either you or your spouse may be more of the caregiver than the other. This usually depends on the circumstances of the connection you each have with your new child. Here is where a word of caution is called for. For example, the child may be a relative of either you or your spouse. Things are changing, time has shifted, and you may not have noticed that one of you, in your solid, sacred partnership, is being neglected.

May I recommend a few things for those of you who were a loving couple – just the two of you – before your new family arrangement? It can feel a bit selfish for you to look back and try to hold on to what life looked like before. But let's look at ways to make sure neglect and/or resentment doesn't creep in. This is a big deal. We are talking about the rest of your life – and this is *extremely* important! No one else is going to step in and help you with this, if you're not proactive in caring for your relationship with each other. I want you to find – not *attempt* to find – a safe person who will come alongside you and help you to have some outings – just the two of you – as a happy couple. At best, you need a good

At best, you need a good date night. I'm recommending that you make time to have dinner out on the town, and then maybe take in a movie or a play.

Take time to nurture your own life, while saving the life of another. You can do this by letting others help you along the way.

date night. I'm recommending that you make time to have dinner out on the town, and then maybe take in a movie or a play. If you're able to, I would stretch it to a weekend trip for the two of you. Visit that favorite B and B; get some time at the lake, the seashore, the mountains or another special place. But be sure to take the time to focus on each other. If you are planning to have your own children, you will need to have these times away to remember your own family planning and romantic needs. Be sure not to neglect each other – and devote some true quality time to connect.

Let's not lose sight of who you were before this added responsibility. I know it's hard to look after yourself in times of need, but you don't want to have any regrets as you make your way through this journey as a referee and caregiver. The "blame game" can pop its ugly head up years later. Don't let what you gave up to help your relative become a wedge between you and your spouse. Let's not have any regrets. Take time to nurture your own life, while saving the life of another. You can do this by letting others help you along the way.

For those of you with children prior to guardianship, I have not forgotten you. Your world has its own set of complications. Depending on the ages of your children, their genders, and the differences in your family values versus those of the guardian child, you are going to deal with huge potential integration issues. Blending everyone together to create a seamless family unit is going to take good communications and patience. An understanding by your own children to help the new guardian child settle in will be imperative. But, with a special note to your children, they need to know from you that you will monitor all of the relationships for any potential hurt feelings for them as they make this sacrifice. At first they may be very eager to help you protect the guardian child – but this could turn to their feeling a bit neglected. This is a huge topic. And in the upcoming chapters, I hope you will find some strategies that you can apply to your own family.

Chapter Recap

The fact that you are now an emerging new family cannot be ignored – it can, now, only be embraced. For those of you without children prior to guardianship, remember now to plan time for just the two of you. Your young marriage, and this new huge commitment, can drain the life out of you. Please plan those special times away. Engage those who can help, and know that they are there to support you. How you decide to structure this arrangement will make or break your new family. Take time to decide how it could look, and shape it as much as you can. I know that we can lay the best plans with thought alone, but the outcome can be completely different. Agreeing to be flexible and make adjustments along the way, is always important. You can review your plan daily if needed, or even sit and share with the whole family if the children are old enough. If you don't plan anything, then you will open yourself up to an unpredictable outcome, where anything could happen. Move forward boldly, measure your results – and plan for success.

Chapter Twelve

Hitting Restart

Most of us have heard the term "restart" as it relates to technology. My phone starts to drag, and my tech-geek son tells me to turn it off and on again. He says, "Dad, you know what to do – I have to tell you this *so* much." Of course, I always forget to do this tiny little detail, yet it is so important. My laptop has the same issue as my phone, with just a different twist to it. I usually don't close out my tabs – and from what I learned from my son, this takes up a lot of memory power. Usually I only remember to restart when my tech stuff begins to run sluggishly, or lock up on me. Life is a lot like this.

In a very fundamental way, we need to hit our own restart button on our guardianship, putting life back into perspective. You have been through the first round – and you have won protective guardianship over your child. This is a time when you are tending to your own wounds after the battle (assuming you had one, and most of us do). Hitting the restart button of your guardianship can be a healthy process. The battle may have clouded your view of why you started down this path in the first place. You need to focus on the main goal here – your love for your guardian child, and your desire to protect them. Start back at the point when you simply had this desire come to the front of your mind. Forget about the battle – and know that it's now over. This will help heal the possible wounds you have from the fight. Also, this allows you to fully engage in the next phase of your guardianship.

Hitting the restart button at any point of your guardianship is amazingly refreshing. You have to give yourself permission to do this. This can only start with you – the guardian – before you can convey this process to your guardian child. Find the time, and find a quiet, comfortable space. I know it's hard to do, but here are a few ideas about how to handle it. Write out your favorite parts of your guardianship, for example, how you feel when you see a complete and protected child — harmony for your child — a child who now has hope, and a future. The last section of *Guardian Shift* has tools to help you design your restart. Once you have written out enough points, reminding yourself of the reasons a good-hearted person like you took a child in under guardianship care, you're halfway to your restart. Review them, and then make any changes needed to reflect your new beginning.

Let's now put them into action. You may be able to restart without telling your child what you are up to. Simply implement changes in your actions to reflect the desired changes you have listed. Make sure you do these steps methodically, and start

120

them ever so slightly. Your child may notice your new actions, depending on your restart goals. They may ask you for clarity. No problem. Just sit down with them and tell them how much you love them, and how much you want to make positive changes to create a new outcome. Tell them you did this to make sure that your whole family was headed toward a deliberate future goal. They will most likely jump in and help you take this new restart mode to new places. Once cool things start happening, you may be caught up in the next mode...

The Honeymoon

There seems to be a euphoria in the air with any new beginning. I call it the "honeymoon phase." Like all honeymoons, though, it will come to an end. That's just life. As you approach the "getting settled in" part of the journey, things can begin to come up that weren't there before. This is due in part to a new level of comfort that you've reached. It is good, although it can sometimes be complicated. I know that our start with our nephew was really rough, with the police having to pick him up and the trauma associated with that, but the good news is that he settled in. What young boy wouldn't like the comforts of food in the fridge and clean clothes to wear?

I am confident that your first show of love was the tough one – and that is the fact that you loved enough to take control of the child's life and chart a new course.

Even if your child's transition is not so dramatic, it is still, most likely, a huge change. They recognize that the change is good, but they may not acknowledge it with you anytime soon. Some will just go through the motions, letting you think they are on board, to buy peaceful time. All types of emotions are in play with your child, and all ages respond differently to the change. One thing I know as a parent is that there is power in showing love. It is a powerful emotion, one that can change lives. It is an emotion that transcends age and issues. The more we use love as we foster this new relationship we have entered into, the more we will see its power. I am confident that your first show of love was the tough one – and that is the fact that you loved enough to take control of the child's life and chart a new course. This is the first known act of love. I believe that if this is executed well, it will show up throughout the restart for you both.

Chapter Recap

Hitting the restart button has many benefits. First, it allows you to get back in touch with the reasons you became a guardian – to provide protection and love for the child. You need to be able to start over sometimes, so that you don't carry any baggage of your own, which could grow into something ugly. It's important that you deal with your wounds early on. You can rediscover the love and joy in what you are doing for this little one. As I look back, I am more convinced than ever that if I had hit my own restart button earlier, I would have avoided some negative thinking. It only hurts the one who holds the pain, so why not give it up and move on? Releasing it takes practice, as well as the ability to overlook the infractions. Forgetting is the next objective. I like to say that we can never totally forget – but we can forget enough to move forward.

Chapter Thirteen

Encouraging Sources

Many guardians have shared with me that they have had a challenge finding the right support people. Sometimes people were not a good fit, or they weren't equipped in the ways the guardians needed them to be. It's not an easy task to come alongside friends and support them through the intense decisions they need to make in guardianship. It is a sensitive issue regarding the best practice in protecting a child. I give credit to anyone who does reach out and help you! We were fortunate that we had a wonderful base of friends. When the situation shook out, they were the ones who became our new family as our relationships with my wife's blood-related family blew to smithereens! Jeannie's family wanted to control how we cared for our nephew – and as you may imagine, they weren't looking out for our nephew's best interest. I am sure that many of you can relate. The friends who came alongside us went above and beyond the call of duty.

I give credit to anyone who does reach out and help you! We were fortunate that we had a wonderful base of friends.

They showed up at court hearings, and they watched our sons while we drove 100 miles each way. This gave us the freedom to do battle while obtaining guardianship of our nephew. They listened to us tell them about the drama (we all have it), and they gave us a safe place to vent. Our friends celebrated with us when we were awarded permanent guardianship. They gave us cards with special notes in them, plus hugs and many supportive phone calls. Most importantly, they cried with us and they rejoiced with us! As our nephew transformed from the tough way of life he had been living, he began to flourish in a more stable and secure life with us. It was as though we had our own little village there to celebrate with us. I could fill this book with personal stories about each one, but I have reserved a place of honor for them in the acknowledgments section – which is *still* not enough for all they did for Jeannie and me.

The following story came from someone who is raising her brother's children. This story, from both the woman and her husband, really touched my heart, and I wanted to include it for you. You will see that she credits her friends for the many ways they reached out to help her family. As you will read, she is a Christian, and she has relied on God in a way that has helped them both through this time of going from no children to a full house with three youngsters. They were simply enjoying life as a married couple, spending all their free time with each other – which instantly became a busy life of immediate parenthood! As you can imagine, it was a *huge* change for them. I hope you enjoy her words of encouragement. Here is her story – in her own words:

About a year ago, my life changed forever. I didn't know it at the time, but what was happening was much more significant than the temporary "crisis management" scenarios I had become used to with my family.

I am the second of five children, and both of my younger brothers have chosen lives outside of God's will. Many of their choices have led to consequences that are difficult and painful, not only for them, but for me and the rest of our family as well. As most people know, we are not islands — and often the ripples from our actions and choices reach much farther than we intend them to, bringing with them results that are more permanent than we ever thought possible.

One of my younger brothers also has a mental-health issue involved — bipolar schizophrenia — that complicates everything further. Often, in a person with mental-health issues, it is difficult to separate the "disease" from just plain bad choices they are making. Usually, in a family, there is that "fixer" person who, over time, becomes the one that the others tend to look to for help in a crisis. Who knows why, exactly, I have become that person in my family. In the last several years I'd begun to learn to set healthier boundaries, and I had tried to keep from constantly being drawn into reaping the unhealthy fruit of their bad decisions.

Last October, my brother — who had moved to Scottsdale with his three young children a year and a half earlier, became homeless, with no idea what he was going to do. He was considering farming out the kids — one to this friend, one to someone else — because he was completely out of options. I begged him to go to the State and tell them he was unable to care for them (for many reasons, including mental-health issues), hopefully to have all of them placed in the same foster home so that the children wouldn't have to be split up. The kids were four, five and six years old, and some of the only consistency in their lives up to that point was having the three of them together as a close family unit.

On Monday, October 26, 2011, a state worker called me at work. They asked if it would be possible for me to pick up the kids after school and daycare, and also to keep them for a few days until they could figure out what to do. This all came about because my brother had gone to them and said that he was unable to care for them. If we couldn't, she told us, they would have to find emergency foster placements. Plus, she told me they wouldn't likely find a home for all three children quickly – or together.

This was a situation that my husband Jonathan and I had half-expected and feared would happen... and I wasn't sure what to tell the state worker. We live in our first home — a very little "starter" home that was the perfect size for the two of us. Where would we even put three kids, even for a short period of time? Jonathan and I had already talked – and we

> *I was so torn! I was falling in love with these kids – and I felt they were going to be ripped from my arms any day.*
>
> *–Amanda, guardian parent*

were on the same page about it – and even though it was heartbreaking, we would not be able to try to keep all three children. But we agreed that they shouldn't be separated, and we reluctantly said yes. We let her know that we could only do it temporarily until they could arrange for a foster family that could take all three of them.

Now, almost a year has passed by. SO much has happened, I could fill a couple of books with stories! I could fill buckets with the tears I have cried in those first few months. The state dragged their feet on doing anything at all, and in the meantime, I was living week to week as an emotional wreck, unsure if this was the last week I would get to snuggle with them on Saturday morning or get to have one more.

They knew clearly that "Daddy was going to be homeless" when we picked them up. They have come from such a heartbreaking life, but we couldn't say "You will be here forever." We were just trying to stitch one day to the next at this point, and make it through. I was so broken during this time – but life required kids to be picked up, teeth to be brushed, work to be done, homework to be finished... and oh, so much more.

It was becoming clear to us as the first few months of our "situation" was playing out that we might be in this for the long haul. We decided to keep the kids, or else they would be placed in a foster home, probably several counties away from their school, their friends, *any familiarity. Knowing that they probably would be far away from us, we feared we wouldn't be able to visit very often. From working in the area of foster care a few years ago, I knew that foster-care placements could be solid, even permanent placements. But usually, there are multiple placements for children as they go through the foster-care system. I was so torn! I was falling in love with these kids – and I felt they were going to be ripped from my arms any day.*

This past year has been the hardest in my life, and also the most difficult of our five years of marriage. My husband Jonathan is... so wonderful, and I believe that God hand-picked him for me. We have the usual compatibilities – I am the extrovert, he is the quiet one. I love the spotlight, usually, but he is much more comfortable filling in the background, or not visible at all. I feel that most of the time, Jonathan lets me have my way, but maybe it's because he's really good at choosing his battles!

Jonathan was clear about our commitment to the children. It was something we could do for a while, but not something he could sign on to for the rest of his life. How could I blame him? It was an impossible situation, with no good options. The kids were being faced with the ugly fallout of their parents' chaos-filled lives. None of this was fair. It wasn't fair to the kids to be in the situation, and it wasn't fair to us. This doesn't change the fact, of course, that they needed a place to be – and someone to take care of them – and that we were the only ones willing to do it.

My heart broke daily as the months went on. Jonathan and I had some of the hardest conversations of our marriage. We seldom fight (remember that part where he usually lets me have my way?) but during these months, some of our discussions were filled with heart-wrenching tension. We agonized over the uncertainty of our lives, and about what our lives would be like if this were the choice we made. We missed what we now looked back upon as "our carefree lives of before." We had no idea how to do what we were being asked to do. There was no one to be mad at, no one to give us any easy answers, no one to take anything off our plate.

Remember when I said I was familiar with dealing with crisis? This meant that for me I was used to "early responder" mode, the way cops and firefighters handle things, where you go into high gear and do whatever needs to be done. You fix the problem – but then the situation subsides, and you move back into "normal" mode. I'm definitely one to jump at something with an emotional reaction – and then try to make decisions before they're completely thought out.

Jonathan, on the other hand, would prefer to have a ten-point plan in place. It helps him make decisions, so that he can weigh his options out and see what, exactly, he's getting

> *All of a sudden, we are learning to be parents! There have been many who have offered us support, funds, and various kinds of help.*
> *—Amanda, guardian parent*

into. When he commits to doing something, he means it – and he follows through. Making a decision to raise three children who are not his own was not a decision he was willing to consider lightly.

Due to my "crisis / early response" emotional reaction, I have had to deal with some times of intense frustration and burnout. It has been hard to adjust from feeling that this was just a crisis to "get through." Now I understand in my heart that this is a much, much bigger picture and longer haul than I had ever thought it would be.

In many ways, life has passed so quickly this year. In late February, temporary custody was granted to us, a few months after we were able to get some financial assistance for the children. The state extends aid to families who care for other family members — which is called kinship care. Ultimately, Jonathan and I have made the decision to raise Trevor, Mia, and Eva ourselves. In the month following the court hearing, we're all hopeful that they will allow us to change from having only temporary custody of the three children to permanent custody. We are praying that it will remain this way until they are grown. All of a sudden, we are learning to be parents! There have been many who have offered us support, funds, and various kinds of help. We are so grateful to all of the ways our friends have reached out, and made sure that we knew we were not alone. We've lost our sanity, "free time," privacy and sleep – but we've gained so much in exchange.

If I could tell you the story of each of these three children, it would break your heart. The places they've come from, the things they learned at an early age, would surprise you. I could fill hours telling you the amazing ways we've seen them change during this past year with us!

They've struggled, fought us and cried – then softened, and learned to trust. They've begun to find out what a family is, and how loving their family is! This has also taught them to understand who God is. Learning that He loves them, and that they are special – this makes them feel safe. Eva has learned that even though we say "we love" each other, we are to love God the most. When she tells me she loves me, she says, "I love you... but I love God the most." To me, knowing that they're little blocks of the foundation being set so that their hearts will someday be given to Jesus – this is the most important desire we have for them. It is eternal! This is what their story is now. It's now our story – and it was all worth it.

I love these kids so much. I know Jonathan does, too. I feel as though sometimes you go TO your mission field – and sometimes it gets dropped in your lap, or on your doorstep. We have so far to go. I pray, as we look back at this time in our lives, that we will see how God guided us to where He wanted us to go. As I look back at my life so far, I see how He has led me up to this point, and I know that if I can get out of the way, He will continue to lead us.

> We are so grateful to all of the ways our friends have reached out, and made sure that we knew we were not alone.
> —*Amanda, guardian parent*

While I was in college, I remember thinking about what I wanted to be and do. The main thing I remember praying for was that my life would make a difference and be significant. We don't want anyone to think we're special, or anything else about our sacrifices, except that God is amazing! He is our provider and WE must trust HIM with our lives. He knows what He is doing and He has a plan for us. There are so many people with stories of their own, and ours is just one of these stories of hope. We wanted to share it with you to encourage you, and to remind each of us to forge on. Shocking as you may think your past or your story is, just share it and let God do with it what He will.

"For I know the plans I have for you," declares the Lord, "plans to prosper you and not to harm you, plans to give you hope and a future."

-Jeremiah 29:11

Chapter Recap

The way this story affects me feels like putting meat tenderizer all over my heart! A look into the sacrifice that these two young people have made is so touching. They went from "Hey, let's go see a movie at 9 p.m." to tucking three little children into bed. And from what I read, it has been a huge transition, but they are loving it. She shared from the heart in a way that we can all relate to. I know that each and every one of you has a unique story of your own. The grandest take-away is the fact that they moved into action, and began to make a difference in the lives of these three children. The role of their friends as "Support People" was inspirational. They stepped in and helped this young couple in so many ways. It's vital that we get all our support people up to speed on our lives as guardians, so that they can better participate in the valuable role they play. The thought of letting the three children go into the foster-care system just broke this couple's hearts. I know that if just one person is encouraged by this story to go out and protect a child, all the ink and paper in the world is well worth it. So grab your bootstraps and saddle up. A child may be waiting for you!

Chapter Fourteen

Family Dynamics and Integration

Integration for families with or without children poses a huge hurdle. As we moved toward bringing another boy into our home, with our three sons, we did what we thought were all the right steps. We had a family meeting to allow each of our sons the opportunity to express his feelings about bringing their cousin to live in our home. Each of them looked at the modifications they could make to provide room, and accept another member into the family as a brother. This, I thought, was very admirable of my sons. They understood the fact that things needed to change for their cousin. However, none of us knew how our lives would be affected. We never really considered the upcoming consequences, only looking at the benefits to our nephew. Our mindset was to protect and provide for our nephew, who was in a crisis. This is the essence of how

It is your job as a parent to make sure that you always help your children to remember how much you love them.

I believe that each of us make that decision to reach out and protect a child. We all have the instinct to protect others from harm – unless you are on the wrong end of that situation.

I think it is important for each of us to consider the shift that occurs when adding to our family. I don't want it to cloud your judgment in making the decision to move forward in protecting a child. I want you to have the encouragement to know there are ways to protect yourselves from the new and changing family dynamics. Let's focus on helping and maintaining your family from this point on. We all need someone to remind us of the goal in this journey. It is to raise and protect your guardian child, while maintaining balance in your own family's life. This is the key, and we didn't see this until we were well into our guardianship journey. It only came when we noticed that our family was out of balance. That was not the greatest of days! I think this was another moment that led us to write this book. We wanted others to be on the lookout for this much earlier in the process than we were. The good news is that you are reading this, and you can make course corrections in your family now, if needed.

There are various ways to look at life, and I have found one that makes sense to me. We are all like little sailboats on the sea. Our goal is to arrive at our destination. When you get to Chapter Twenty-Eight, you will see how I came about learning the following insight. No sailboat ever goes in a straight line. It has to keep tacking back and forth, to ensure that the sails stay full of air. This constant course correction ensures that the sailboat continues to move closer to its destination. *Your* journey cannot be complete without course correction along the way either. I know if someone had come alongside us and said, "Hey, you guys are neglecting your own sons to save your nephew," this would have hit us squarely, and painfully, in the face. We love our sons, and we never wanted that to happen, but unfortunately we did have those moments – and we're not proud of them. Fortunately, we quickly did a course correction in this area, and my goal is for you to avoid ever having to seek that same adjustment – or perhaps to avoid experiencing it in the first place.

Some of you have a full house already. You have your own children, then you mix in your guardian child, and a huge "Shift" occurs in your family dynamics. The coolest part at first is to see the ways that your own children are willing to share. They open their home to make room for the new member, and they are excited to do so. Your family members want the new addition to have the same security and protection that they themselves enjoy. When they open their worlds up to the new child, plus fully open to share their own Mom and Dad, it is huge! Your own children believe in you so much that they want to share *you,* so that you can then make a difference for their cousin. What an honor to know that your children feel this way about you. It comes with a price for each one of you, as everyone has a different investment in your family's journey. The first thing that can happen as you let your children help in the integration process with your niece or nephew is the sharing of their friends. Over time, jealousy can set in, for either your child or your guardian child.

Your children's friends may have been tipped off already that your family would be expanding. Your children make preparations to welcome and include their cousin, and they're waiting with excitement for his or her arrival. As the sharing begins, you and your family are now embarking on a new course. Some of the struggles could be that your children's friends may not accept your new family member, or they simply don't have the same interests. Whatever the case, people will give you their feedback even when you don't ask for it. Once the integration phase with the new family member is well underway, then new family dynamics start to appear. Jumping back to to the scene of preschoolers playing on the floor together (from Chapter Eleven), you may have to step in and redirect a selfish spirit or two. You may well need to calm struggles on topics you never thought you were going to have to handle – and sometimes this is even shocking. I will address more of that later in the teen series, on unpacking the garbage and repacking their bag with success tools for life.

After your guardianship has progressed well past the integration phase, you will be due for some family maintenance. Your family will reflect a bit of how things used to be; not dwelling on it, but now seeing the effects of the changes you have been through. It is your job as a parent to make sure that you always help your children to remember how much you love them. You must commend them for the sacrifices they have made to make this Guardian Shift happen. Without them, you could never have set sail on this journey to make a difference in another life.

Here are a few ideas to make your own children feel that they are a big part of the process. You know their interests in life. Take each one out to do one-on-one activities with them that you and they can enjoy together, creating memorable moments for everyone. Make a conscious effort to connect with them, and thank them for their support and their generous, giving heart. Acknowledging them will go miles! They don't need to be babied along the way – they simply need to know that you see what they gave to make the "Shift" happen. Let them know they are a huge part in making the much-needed difference in the life of another. You will feel loved by them for the sacrifice you made also, which may have led to a sense of your own children not having enough of you. Tell them some of the ways that you saw them making sacrifices. This will make them feel especially good. Dads, you may want to plan a "daddy and daughter" date night. You could take her to a nice restaurant, to simply spend quality time together. Moms, you may want to take your sons out to a movie they like, showing them that you too are interested in what they are interested in.

The main point here is to spend some quality time, one on one, with your biological children. Make them feel loved for the investment they have made to make a difference in the life of your guardian child. This is especially important if there is one parent who is out of balance. If one of you is investing the majority of time for the guardian child, you may need to shift some quality time to your own children. One of you may be the primary go-to person more than the other one. This will show your children, even though there's been a shift in the family dynamics, that you still have time for them.

Chapter Recap

Integrating a new member into the family can have its challenges at times. It's human nature to overcompensate to help a child in guardianship adjust, and this can create a possible imbalance within your own family. Everyone is eager to help in protecting the new member. But it is our responsibility to maintain balance, and the emotional well-being of our family.

Make sure that the sacrifice your family puts into bringing a child into your home is always respected. Your family members may not expect to be recognized – but I recommend that you do it anyway. A new world opens up to your whole family when we seek harmony. Balance will resume, and more giving will come to the front of everyone's mind. Adults and children alike respond to being appreciated, so morale rises. Your family will be strong, and your task of integrating your new child will return to a state of balance. Every member now feels loved in the way they need to be. Remember that all those course corrections keep the wind in your sails to make a difference. Sail on!

Chapter Fifteen

Social Media

As with any other area of our lives, we need to check up on our social media intake and outflow. What we post is important, but perhaps even more important is what you let your child in guardianship consume on social media. Some people live their lives right out on social media for all to know. They post when they have a headache, and they post some new selfie that they took at the mall. They will tell you about the traffic jam they may be in, or if they are having coffee in some popular area. Is any of this wrong? No. My goal here is not to condemn any of it. But it's important to see if it could adversely affect the new role that you play as a guardian. In 2003, our children had just received their first cell phones. Nowadays, a cell phone is essentially a pocket computer, and with the touch of a finger it allows access to anything. It's almost unstoppable, unless you disconnect the service – and even this becomes difficult with today's easy access to wifi. Time spent online is no longer limited to the time you let your children use the computer in the study!

I am sure, however, that some control still remains after we have given our child a smart phone. I know that some boundaries have to be established, along with guidelines of transparency. In short, full-access look into the social media they are involved with is a great solution, if we can arrive at this. Access to the passwords they use is essential, enabling you to have an accountability check.

Yikes! I almost pulled my hair out just writing that last line. Jeannie and I are raising Gracie (she's eight years old now) and we are going to have to deal with this for her as well – sooner than we think! We will have the challenge also of navigating this phase in a fast-moving environment that didn't exist when we raised our sons. We're going to need some help! We do have the luxury, though, of building those values gradually. If you are just slammed into it, and have not had the time to build the framework of values to build trust, it may be difficult.

Trust has to be created – and there has to be a method for earning the privilege of having a phone.

First of all, a phone is a luxury, not a necessity. Yes, it is a safety tool, but when you have yet to deal with your new child in this manner, you have to use caution. Trust has to be created – and there has to be a method for earning the privilege of having a phone. So time is on your side in this regard. Attitude always has a way of gaining good things or losing them. I recommend watching the child's grades to see if they are finishing their assignments, scoring well on exams, and earning good grades overall. Most schools allow you to see what your child has been assigned, and when the due dates are. This will help you to monitor the truth when it comes to "Do you have any homework?" and to check them on timelines. You didn't have the time to build the trust gradually, so you have to find ways to do it

When people have nothing but the truth coming from them, they are usually very calm and open.

that will make sense to your child as well as to you. They will want the phone immediately, but I recommend that you build up to it. Once they have shown that they have been honest with you, and that they are getting the grades you've agreed on, you'll have something to work with.

Next, you have to see how their interaction within the family is going. Getting good grades is just part of it – the other part is to see how they are treating others. This is such an important part of the puzzle, and when you see how they treat others, it shows who they truly are. If you want to peer into their hearts, look at this area first – it always tells the deeper story. When people have nothing but the truth coming from them, they are usually very calm and open. When they have something to hide, it is quite the opposite. Ask a few random times to look at their phones, and see what reaction you get. Remind them of the terms you originally laid out for the use of this privilege.

Chapter Recap

Media pounds technology use into this crazy world we live in. Your toughest job will be how to monitor their media intake. We cannot control the billboards they see, or what they hear in the world around them, but we can control the phones, computers and television to a degree. How you do this will determine how well you set the stage of "Why?" – which is vitally important to your child's well-being. It may take several conversations to build the concept of "Garbage In, Garbage Out" – and once they determine why this is important, it will become easier. It's just like junk food. Sometimes you just don't feel good after eating it – and if you keep eating it, on a prolonged basis, unpleasant results begin to show up. Put good things into their minds, and this will produce good things in their lives.

Chapter Sixteen

What Do I Call You?

This topic pulls on heartstrings for everyone involved. When you pour your heart into being a mom or a dad to your new child, emotions are high. You are fully engaged in protecting and nurturing their lives from the beginning. Well then, why aren't you "Mom" or "Dad"? You ought to be, right? Those bozos (their birth parents) had their chance already! Hold your horses there, though, before you think I'm not on your bandwagon for this topic. I most certainly am. This subject has many moving parts – and it's not so easy to quickly determine the best solution.

Depending on the age of the child, you have some different ways they will see this. The older the child, the more a very new emotion sets in. It's called betrayal. This is where we will begin, and then we'll work our way down to the younger ones. I can tell you from experience how this played out for us. My nephew loved me like a father, but my commitment was to never

Remember one thing: if they are old enough to be concerned about their biological parents, they are smart enough to love and respect you like a father or mother for the life and foundation you are giving them.

take away the title of his own father. Even though my nephew never had a mother in his life – and Jeannie was like a mother to him, after his grandmother – he rarely called her mom. We touched lightly on the subject, and found that "Auntie" and "Uncle" were our titles. That was his choice, and that was fine. Occasionally, our nephew simply forgot he'd come from somewhere else, and let his guard down. Sometimes we'd hear the occasional "Mom" or "Dad," but this was coming from a wholly relaxed state of mind. Sometimes the hopes of a child's original family coming back together is in the back of their minds, and it is not our right to take it from them – no matter how bad the situation was that they came from. Over time, it will get more clear to them as to how they want to address you. Remain confident that they know who cares for them now. *That* is what's most important!

If betrayal is even remotely in the mind of your child, I would respect their feelings. If you are good with "Auntie," "Uncle," "Grandma" or "Grandpa," then I think you are a winner! Remember one thing: if they are old enough to be concerned about their biological parents, they are smart enough to love and respect you like a father or mother for the life and foundation you are giving them. You will always love them like a son or daughter, and this will always shine beyond mere titles. Give them their space, and let them open the doorway to love and address you as they wish. They know who has given them this chance to live a right life. You may not feel the love today, but one day your hearts will connect and you will know it.

Now for the younger ones. This is fun, because they don't have the capacity to know betrayal. The only way this emotion begins to show its ugly little head is when the biological parents plant those seeds (perhaps with other relatives chiming in). I can only express the biggest warning possible about this behavior. It is destructive, and unwarranted, for the bio-parents to do this! Let's go back to our motto, "Guardians guard," and let the bio-parents know that this is not happening on your watch. The bio-parents (please note that I have now removed the "logical" part of the term), want to feel that they are still loved, even after they have lost their child. In my opinion, they are very insecure at this point. If they are remotely in touch with their loss, insecurities will develop. They have lost a child, and they want to have *some* authority as a parent, but it's no longer possible. Once you let them get away with undermining you, it can become a cancer and repeat itself in other areas. So let's nip it in the bud! They need to come to the conclusion quickly that at this point, they are to put the welfare of the child first, and not their own emotional or irrational feelings. The identity of the guardian who makes decisions for the child has now "Shifted."

Let's have some fun now with titles. You and your little ones, or even the bigger kids, can create names for you. For example, I could have been "Uncle S," or Jeannie could have been "Auntie J," but we never chose that route. I know a family who has helped with three children of friends, and they call the mom there "Mommy-Nay," which is cute and doesn't infringe on the bio-mom. This originated from my friends real name, Renee. It all works for them. The best

Being a mother or a father is not a matter of shared DNA.

part is that adults find it cute – at least I do – and sometimes I call her that too, just for fun. Grandparents are part of a family lineage, as much so as a mother and father, so "Grandma" and "Grandpa" are, I feel, spot on. Of course, I have heard many cute names for grandparents too.

Names and titles are also an issue in step-families, where there is a step-mom or step-dad. I have a friend who lived with her father and step-mom but saw her mom on a regular basis. The dad wanted her to call the step-mom "Mom," but the daughter felt that since she already had a mom, that would be disrespectful to her own mother. Her relationship with her bio-mom, in her mind, was being compromised. I know the issue of step-families is something else entirely, but the point is that if the child had even a small relationship with the bio-parent, they could feel it to be disrespectful or wrong to call you, as their guardian, "Mom" or "Dad." So you have to see where they are on this topic, as every situation is different. There is no pat answer as to how to address you. But don't sweat it. You know that *you* are the "Mom" or "Dad" figure to them.

Chapter Recap

Have fun, I say, with names! Don't demand a title! Allow one to be offered, then sealed upon you. This will remove tons of stress for both you and your child. If it means that they want to call you by your first name, you will need to be the judge of this. My take on first names is that it's a way for the child to potentially cope. You are a hero to them already – you don't need any particular name badge to go along with it. Being a mother or a father is not a matter of shared DNA. The recognition goes deeper than a name. It's the fact that in their heart, children know what a mother or father is, and does. In every way, deep down inside, they feel the love of a mother or father by the way you care for them. If they cannot pay you the respect of using "Mother" or "Father" as your title, just know that the recognition will show up in other ways. Many times it will be felt in the way that they trust you for everything. This is especially rewarding, because you know that they would never do this with their bio-parent. So carry on, knowing that you are loved from somewhere deep in their little hearts – just as you should be. Love is *felt* in many more ways than it may be *spoken!*

Chapter Seventeen

Reconciling Equals Love

Children in guardianship are some of the most forgiving people I have ever seen. They have survived more battles in their young lives than you and I can imagine, especially the older ones. Some have seen things that I won't write about. Many have lived in horrific conditions and endured indescribable heartache and pain. You would think that reconciling would be the last thing on their minds – but you and I would be wrong. Now, don't assume that I am talking about the child returning to the bio-parents – I am not. I am talking about a point in time where either the child or you will reconcile, and commit to working on the damaged relationships with the child's parents. All of this will happen *only* if the bio-parents are in a place to do so as well.

I can almost feel you slamming the book closed right now. Please don't. Read on with me, and if you don't agree, we will be on to a new topic in a few pages. Thank you! Work with me for a few rounds. If reconciliation is needed, you will know. The feeling you could be stuck in may be bitterness, or a nagging voice to clear the potential matter up. Bitterness is the cancer of all cancers, and it can cause so many problems. If you are harboring this vile little emotion, I want you to know this: you are the only one it is hurting! It is tearing *you* up more than the one who helped to put it there. It will eat your bones away and cloud your judgment for the future. You can find so many published articles out there on the subject that will confirm this for you – don't just take my opinion.

This in no way says you're giving up control – just that you're willing to forgive, and work on a better future.

One thing I know for sure is that your example sets the tone for the child in your care. I can tell you that when I took a stand to work out the differences with our nephew's father, my popularity rating went up with my nephew. Now, was I sharp enough to see it at the moment? Well, it took a while, and I finally got it when my nephew actually thanked me for taking the time to work on the relationship. This was extremely moving for all of us. In the beginning, the amount of effort it took was huge – and it was draining! I knew I was showing love to my nephew by working on my relationship with his father. So, if you decide to swallow your pride, I feel you will be rewarded for it. This in no way says you're giving up control – just that you're willing to forgive, and work on a better future. Doing this will speak volumes to your guardian child, and maybe even motivate them to perform to levels not yet reached.

Have you ever had a child ask you to look at the picture they just colored? You can feel how important it is for them to see and hear your approval. Children in guardianship want you to not hate their bio-parents, even though one or both of the parents may deserve it. In many cases, the child in your care still wants their bio-parent(s) to approve of them. This seems to be some rite of passage that a child needs to progress into adulthood. I never said this part was easy, but it is most definitely rewarding. Letting go of bitterness has many health benefits, as well as the mental relief that you all will feel. You will now be able to move into a world in which you could grow your relationship with the bio-parent. I recommend that you first meet with the bio-parent privately; this will begin the reconciling process just between the two of you. There's no sense in having a garbage-dumping match in front of the child. *No one* wins that way. These reconciliation meetings may be the framework to encourage the bio-parents to get their act together. This is way beyond the call of duty for you, I know, but it will prove that you went the extra mile, beyond any doubt.

Maybe you have already had one or more meetings with the bio-parents. Hopefully, you may have become more civil in your interaction with them by now. Some healing may have already taken place, and you may be ready to open the door to share what you and your guardian child have been up to. It's scary, yes! I want you to assure the child, though, that you didn't do this in order to return them to their parents, but to give them a chance at reconciliation and healing. If they are unwilling, or feeling spooked in any way by this, by all means drop

Taking the high road is not the easiest path – that's why it's the high road.

Reestablishing relationships and ridding yourself of bitterness is healing. It will keep your head clear to speak, and to make good decisions.

the subject until further notice. They may have more to deal with than you think. If they jump at the opportunity, then I say you should support them in it. Explain that this will only happen if they remain civil, and not get physical. Now if they want to yell... well, I am not 100% against this, as long as they dial it back after a bit. Does your child need to vent? Well, you will find out at the meeting. Encourage them to use these times to get it all out.

When we began our own healing process with our nephew and his dad, some pain and anger were involved. This too was helpful to us, as it bonded our relationships as guardians. If you are insecure about how to set up a reconciliation meeting, or set of meetings, I recommend that you contact a counselor to help you. Do this until you have reached a stage in your relationship when you can start to facilitate the meetings on your own. Call around to find someone who can mediate until you can all be in the same room without tension getting the better of anyone. Remember that you have been in protection mode, and that you have learned more than you cared to about past issues. If you let it, this could cause you to bite some heads off and sabotage the whole process.

Okay, so you have either read through the last few pages or you just flipped ahead. Let's talk about the love again, as seeking reconciliation can be the biggest act of love in reaching some common ground with your child's bio-parents. Doing this says to the child, "You are important to me even if my own son or daughter, brother or sister has upset me." Taking the high road is not the easiest path – that's why it's the high road. When you start down this path, don't rush things. Take your time, and if no positive ground is made, then just stop. You can always make another run on it at a later point – what counts is the fact that you tried. I must admit that after we made an effort to right the wrongs in our situation, my wife and I both felt that we had gained better control of our emotions. We discovered this by trial and error, and we wanted to share this as an option for you to use. Making peace has its benefits, and showing that you're willing to move toward it is a *big* step! Now if the other party is not ready, or not mature enough, this becomes an entirely different story. You may have bio-parents who are so stuck on themselves that they can't see that they did anything wrong. This is hard to deal with, but please realize that it will make you stronger if you try. Don't expect them to rise to the occasion, because they may not be able, for whatever reason, to do so. You are the ones on the high road, and if they are going to take potshots at you, don't let them hurt you. If you have to go back to the day when the bio-parent you are looking at was your sibling growing up, then do so. Just know that you may still be able to reach them, somewhere in the dysfunction that they are currently living in.

Chapter Recap

Reestablishing relationships and ridding yourself of bitterness is healing. It will keep your head clear to speak, and to make good decisions. Letting go is for you – and this is the biggest way for you to teach the child in your care how to forgive and move on. Please don't misunderstand me; reconciling is no way an admission of weakness. It's way at the other end of the spectrum, in fact – it's immensely powerful, and it can create a sense of freedom. Hold on to the thought of being, and staying, in control of your emotions, as well as the fact that *you* are creating the outcome of how someone will potentially treat you in the future. Showing love to your guardian child may speed recovery in ways we can't imagine, or predict. Take the risk — it may have rewards far beyond your beliefs!

Chapter Eighteen

Swooping "Bios" — Phone Calls and Holidays

This is a time bomb that has no mercy. You know – the times when your adult child or your brother or sister makes a cameo visit – especially when it's unexpected. Then "Bio" (your guardian child's bio-parent) attempts to create the illusion that they are doing great – which confuses your guardian child, causing the child to think, "Why am I not living with you?" These moments cause damage that can take hours, days or even weeks to recover from. I have seen more hurt in the visits that we guardians allow to take place than you can imagine. You have engaged your heart and soul in protecting this child, and "Super-Bio-Parent" shows up as though nothing is wrong! They attempt to win over the child's heart, trying to prove they are still a good parent. Ouch! Painful! Yes! That hurt runs down the inside of your arm like the warning sign of a heart

You have engaged your heart and soul in protecting this child, and "Super-Bio-Parent" shows up as though nothing is wrong!

attack. Your child just "goes gaga" over the visit, and thinks that "Super-Bio-Parent" is so great. Right? I am addressing this painful moment because your feelings get hurt, and no one really understands *why* this hurts so much. Our friends and families all tell us to consider the source, right? Even if the source is dysfunctional, the heart of the child in your care just got snapped – which, in some cases, generates a false hope. Your guardian child may have some hidden hope that Mom or Dad will come back to save the day. This is *not* happening – and we all know it! Now you are stuck nursing the wounded heart of this little one back to reality after the visit. And that's not easy!

This can cause some of the work you have done to come undone. You may have to settle your child down once again. So the visit may have lasted just an hour or two, but you are left with what could be days of behavioral issues to manage. Some of you have said that the sassy attitude is more than you bargained for and that you would love to undo the visit. Then the bio-parents wonder why you may not be able to make the next scheduled visit in *their* chosen time frame. They don't understand why you need to set some boundaries and guidelines on how the visit should flow.

They're oblivious to how all of this affects the child. Then they get angry as you attempt to tell them why this is counterproductive. I know it's amazing and hard to comprehend the lack of understanding that the bio-parents show as to why this is harmful to the child. The older the child, and the more able they are to use words to express themselves, the more helpful this is to both you and them. Even though the older ones are able to communicate their feelings, you will still see the pain of reality over the next few days. Once the visit and its effects fully set in, you may be able to talk with the child and find out what they may have felt. Remember that they will only hear you if they feel you are coming from a position of love. You have to know that their hearts are breaking, even though they know they're in the best place they could be. Geez, I am in tears right now as I reflect on those sobering moments of truth with my nephew. I know you will be a superstar, and that you will show your guardian child love – and also, respect for their feelings. I want to encourage you to set those needed boundaries.

The worst is when you have worked so hard to set up a visit, and then the bio-parent is a no-show! I have to say that this is worse than the "Swoop In" visit. This one just screams to the guardian child, "You have no value," and it's tremendously painful. Very simply, it feels to your child like one more punch in the face. Not much can be said about this too quickly; it won't help. Sometimes a loving silence is the best way to communicate, especially if you offer a shoulder or a hug. It's painful for the child – and, once again, the bios just don't get it. They are caught up in themselves, as usual – and *you* are left holding the child's broken heart. A word of caution here: bad-mouthing the bio-parent won't do any good. If you can, move on to another activity and get everyone's mind off the topic. This is my recommendation.

Some of you may have a chronic "visitation villain." Let me explain. These are the bios who regularly miss their scheduled visitation appointments. You're going to have to set some higher standards for these bios. You may be able to just write it out for them – or perhaps they could receive it better if someone else speaks to them. They cannot just continue to stomp on the child's heart – or yours for that matter – anymore. These wounded children want so much to have the approval of their bio-parents that they will go to great lengths to achieve it. Some of the children are willing to overlook their own pain and suffering. Try to watch for this, and let your guardian child know that the bio-parents are doing the best they can with the lives they are currently leading. It is very hard to explain to children that their parents don't have the capacity to parent them.

Phone Calls And Holidays

As I sit here writing, I have just turned my calendar to December. I can remember how phone calls and special dates always created a bit of anxiety with our nephew – and with us too. Looking back, I can now say that I wouldn't have done it any differently. Your intuitive first reaction, nine times out of ten, is going to lead you to the correct path. Your job as a guardian, I repeat, is to guard. And this can be a very difficult position to be in.

It seems like a simple thing to let your guardian child visit on the phone with the bio-parents, "just saying hello." We thought this too, at first, but later found that it caused a great deal of agitation. After doing this from time to time, over about ninety days, we could see a pattern of agitation for a few days leading up to the day of the call, and for about a week afterwards. It dawned on us that this was directly related to the calls, so we started making slow adjustments. Wanting to minimize the highs and lows, we just focused on the positive points, reviewing them daily, and regularly giving our nephew praise for his accomplishments in both school and daily life.

They don't understand why you need to set some boundaries and guidelines on how the visit should flow. They're oblivious to how all of this affects the child.

When we first became guardians in 2003, during the early stages of cell phones and internet, it was a bit easier to control communications. Today, there are so many ways in which cyber connections can occur, especially for teenagers. As I mentioned earlier in the chapter on social media, if your teen has a cell phone, it would be best if there were rules attached to the privilege. This is not easy to do, and the fine line of being firm with cell phone use, and how communications need to flow – coupled with maintaining trust with your teen – can be quite difficult. When the bio-parents feel they have a right to communicate with the child, the cell phone is a direct pipeline. Helping both the bio-parents and your child in guardianship to understand the importance of healing before resuming regular or unplanned communications is difficult. How you get there will involve watching the child's behavior patterns. If they smooth out for longer periods of time between calls, then you will be able to point this out to both the child and the bio-parent.

The bio-parents don't realize how much agitation the child endures after a contact. The bios care only about one thing – themselves! So how do we handle the child? It's easy if they don't bring it up… but, we both know that it's going to happen. If they do, and if you already have a platform of being able to talk about these matters, this makes it easier. Now this is just for the span of time while we're all focusing on creating a smooth integration into everyone's new family dynamics. What we found with the older children is that most of all, they want to feel protected by you. They understand that including parts of their old life can bring instability to their new living conditions. We are grateful that we saw it early on!

For you, the guardian, it can be hard to feel in control of your new role. Taking on the responsibility of someone else's child is a big load, and you are a really brave soul. Those family members who want to tell you what's best for the situation do mean well most of the time. For you, at this time, the focus must be on the child – not the dysfunctional family. Tune out the noise of the ones poking their noses into your new family dynamics – and be a guardian, guarding and protecting your child!

> *Tune out the noise of the ones poking their noses into your new family dynamics – and be a guardian, guarding and protecting your child!*

Let those who seem to know best – and who try to tell you how to do your job – that you've got this. Now, for some of you, this will work just fine. Others will have some cranky relatives to deal with. Go big on this. I mean, stand your ground no matter what. They are not telling you how to raise your *own* children, right? So it's not appropriate for them to offer their input, or for you to accept it, as to how to care for your guardian child. This is especially true, in light of the fact that *you* were the one awarded the guardianship and not *them*. Stand firm, and let them know lovingly, if possible, that when you need their input or assistance, you will call on them. Those who want to tell you how to do your job as a guardian need to *earn* that right first. Let's make sure that they are helping you to hold up the values you have set – or they may have to "go on the naughty list." You may have to put *them* on the supervised visitation list also. And since they might arrange meetings and calls behind your back – which is really destructive – make sure to be on your guard.

Those special dates in life, like birthdays and Christmas, are especially tough. The bio-parents seem to think that these days are for them to make a special impact – or what they may think of as a "show of love." This can really spin the child's mind around – and they could see the bio-parent as loving, and able to care for them again. For others, this only occurs after a long period of time has passed with no contact from the bio-parent. Of course, *you* know that the bio-parent has been caught up in some unsavory lifestyle – and now they want to show up for the big events. Ugh! Some of them, in fact, are downright evil about their intention when they show up on the scene again. Their motivation may seem pure on the surface, but money – or something else that's selfish or guilt-driven – is their main objective. Of course, *you* have to be the mastermind in sorting this all out.

If you can, set a precedent from the start, or begin to make corrections now as to how you handle these special days. This would be best. You are sharing and integrating your values and family life with your guardian child, and there is no room for the bio-parent to disrupt that. You could, if you decide to – out of the goodness of your heart – invite the bio-parent after the holidays are over. If you do it before the holidays, in my opinion, your child's well-being will be affected by the potential agitation from the bio-parent's visit. If the visit doesn't go well, you could jeopardize your whole family's enjoyment of this special season. So if you can, do it afterwards. Explain to the bio-parent that it's about the child, not about them!

One more thing you might consider adding to the mix of connecting with the bio-parent(s) is fair treatment for all. When the bio-parent comes for a holiday visit, they must bring equal-value gifts for your whole family – including your children, you and your spouse. Oh, they may cry that they can't afford it. But if you can get them to do this, it sends a great message to the child in your care that the bio-parent cares about all of you. It shows the child that the bio-parent isn't upset about their child being with you. This may be hard for everyone, but the guardian child needs as much affirmation as they can get that the bio-parent is happy with this arrangement.

In so many cases, all the bio-parent wants to do is make a grandstand show of "how great they are." This is not only not acceptable behavior, it actually sends the wrong message to the child. However you accomplish this, you need to do it for these special days, so that you can make quality memories with your guardian child. It's your job to protect and balance the child and your home – *not* to worry, at all, about the bio-parents' feelings. We are way beyond worrying about how they feel at this point, even though some around you will disagree. It is not your job to make them happy, unless *you* want to. They have conducted themselves in a manner that has changed the course of *your* life – and that is beyond the obvious effects on the child's life. The bio-parents need to wake up and smell the coffee – and realize, once and for all, that they have affected many around them.

Chapter Recap

Remember, guardians are *guards!* With this at the forefront of your decision making, you will succeed in managing contacts, phone calls and holidays. The bio-parents are the ones who have put everyone into this situation – not you! As guardians, we have to remain strong and protect the emotions of the children in our care, even when doing so may make us less popular. You are going to need to rely on people close to you to support your decisions around making the right choice for the child. We cannot stress over the one scenario that makes everyone feel good. Sorry – I couldn't say this any differently. Just remain in control, and push back on the swooping bio-parent. If the bio-parent is ever going to understand the fact of what they have created here, you are going to be the one to teach them. You've got this! You are a warrior!

Chapter Nineteen

Tough Choices

From cover to cover, here in **Guardian Shift,** we have discussed the tough decisions that guardians face. It truly is not a secret that we make a lot of difficult judgment calls while parenting someone else's child. You're faced with doing the best for the child in your care, plus the potential fallout from those close to you and the child. Those tough calls started on the day you decided to obtain guardianship, and they simply keep coming. Healthcare choices need to be made; plus school life, mental-health care, behavioral decisions, extended-family management decisions – and the list goes on and on.

I would like to spend some time on the children who have tough choices of their own to make. Let's take into account that a child, too, has to make choices. From the young ones who are aware of their situation to the teenagers who are *extremely* aware of it, they all have to make tough choices. The most basic one, in

Those tough calls started on the day you decided to obtain guardianship, and they simply keep coming.

my opinion, is when the guardian child simply accepts the new living arrangement and shift in guardians. Moving forward, the guardian child is now faced with deciding on choices that are good for their life, and setting aside how his or her bio-parents may feel. Decisions in the mind of the guardian child could conflict with how bio-parents may react – and now, with how you, their new guardian, will react. This could cause some confusion in how they handle some of their tougher choices.

Sometimes we saw mood changes in our nephew, and we didn't know where they had come from. In a few of those changes it was, in fact, a fear of how Jeannie and I would react to something he was struggling with. He felt that we might respond the same way as his bio-parent would. Once we understood this, we were able to explain that this was a false line of thinking, but I want to clarify that in his mind there was nothing false about it. It was, and is, very real. There were many reasons for our nephew's confusion, and I am sure that many of you can surmise at least some of them. I will leave it at that.

In the following story about my friend Kyle Johnson, you will see how, starting at an early age, he had to make some very tough choices. He had to handle some hard truths, and make choices that were extremely difficult. Those choices began as early as age nine, and they continued through his teenage years. I am sure that his ability to move forward to a more positive life, no matter how much it hurt, will touch you.

Kyle is the father of four sons, and happily married to Christine. I first came into contact with him when our wives met on Facebook. (The ladies, too, have remained in contact ever since.) We met with the Johnsons one afternoon for a very long lunch. During those several hours, Kyle began to tell his story. I found that he had really not shared his story much before this, but I wanted to tell it to you to encourage you. I am going to share with you the trials of his life, before he was able to make it into a guardianship relationship with his aunt and uncle at the age of fifteen.

Let me tell you his story…

Kyle's life before he reached guardianship is filled with what he calls "Environment Abuse." I think it is important to share that he once had a very stable home life. His father was an oil-field worker who earned a good living. Kyle actually remembers his mom and dad buying a nice home for the family.

Then, when Kyle reached the age of six, the oil business fell apart. His daddy looked for work and couldn't find any. This led him to do things that were not good choices. Kyle's daddy then moved away, leaving behind Kyle's mother to support Kyle and his two siblings. Daddy left no money, nor did he contact them for years to come. Mom lost the house and worked as a waitress to provide for herself and the children. Then, as his mother developed a bad habit of meeting the wrong men, she became a victim of abuse over and over. She provided well for the children for the next few years, until Kyle reached the age of nine. Then his mother met the wrong guy, and their drinking turned into a runaway train. Parties at the house kept the children up, sometimes until 4:00 a.m., giving them only a few hours of sleep before school started.

Kyle became the responsible one in the family at the age of nine, and he also became his mom's protector. He remembers getting into the middle of one of the beatings she was taking, only to get kicked. He shared that it was very painful for him to watch the men abuse his mother. The parties became more and more frequent, creating chaos for Kyle and his siblings. At one point, his mother moved them closer to other family members. He had never met these relatives before, and his mom changed his name to Kyle Tidwell. He didn't think much of this, until his cousins started telling him that his daddy was Tom Tidwell and not Robert Johnson, as he'd grown up believing. This created much confusion for Kyle. He eventually met his real dad, but his real dad, Tom Tidwell, wanted nothing to do with him. At the time of this writing, Kyle has yet to contact his bio-dad to ask why he didn't want him. I could see the pain in his face, and I felt the hurt in his heart.

After several years, Robert Johnson, the man Kyle thought was his father, came back into his life. They began with summer visits, and Robert Johnson rekindled interest in him. Kyle, as I stated, had been dealing with parties, drinking and men abusing the only true parent he had, his mom. This pain ran deep, and Kyle really wanted, like any other kid, to go fishing and do things like a kid, but had never had the chance. By this time, his dad – or should I say, the man he thought was his dad – did have some stability in his home, and he had remarried. The summer visit turned into a situation with Kyle not wanting to go back to the environment that his mother had waiting for him. Kyle had come to a decision. He could not take watching the the men in his mother's life abuse her, or her heavy drinking. He loved her, and to this day, he still loves her.

So, at the age of twelve, he made the hardest call he had ever made – the call that would eventually break both their hearts. He told his mother that he loved her, but that he wanted to live with his daddy Robert Johnson. Unfortunately, Robert's new wife really did not care much for Kyle, and she was verbally abusive to him. One solace for Kyle was to go down the street and visit with his Uncle Jacob and Aunt Melanie. They were about seven years older than Kyle, and had no children at the time. Kyle enjoyed doing things with them.

This all seemed to be working out well, for Kyle's freshman year of high school. He had his own bedroom, and he got involved in playing school sports. His grades began to improve – and then disappointment and abandonment came his way again. Kyle's dad and his wife got into trouble and landed up in jail, leaving fifteen-year old Kyle to attempt to bail them out. "Daddy" told Kyle to sell the van and give the money to the bail bondsman. This was not the sort of task a fifteen-year-old boy should be handling. But Uncle Jacob then gave Kyle some help, since Robert was his brother. They were able to get Robert and his wife out of jail, and soon afterward, "Daddy" (Robert) and his wife moved away, leaving Kyle on his own. Uncle Jacob and Aunt Melanie took in this fifteen-year-old, abandoned boy – and you would assume correctly that he was not even their blood. Kyle didn't hear from his father (Robert) again for the next seven years.

=====================

Let's take into account that a child, too, has to make choices. From the young ones who are aware of their situation to the teenagers who are extremely aware of it, they all have to make tough choices.

=====================

Kyle recalls his mom telling him at an early age, "Son, if you want something, you are going to have to work for it." She modeled this for him for his first nine years, before the drinking and abuse came to be a daily event. This lesson stuck for Kyle, and it helped him to develop a good work ethic. For the next five years, Kyle built a great foundation, now modeled by his aunt and uncle. They became his guardians, but in an informal way, not by court appointment. It was one of those events where everyone just let it happen. They loved him and cared for him like he was their own.

When Kyle told me about his relationship with his aunt and uncle, you could see him light up. He shared that while he was living with his aunt and uncle, Uncle Jacob was strong and fair. Aunt Melanie was loving and nurturing. They gave Kyle a chance to have balance in his life, and they modeled being a mom and dad to him. Kyle got to have his own room, and he grew up peacefully for those five years. They helped him get a job and taught him to be responsible. He saved his money. They were awesome role models. Kyle went on to a career in technology, and he now works as an engineer for a major computer company.

Kyle's aunt and uncle now play a huge role for his four sons, and they remain in constant contact with them. They are continuing to model for Kyle, right down to his offspring, playing the roles of grandparents. Uncle Jacob and Aunt Melanie are life changers, in that the role they played as guardian parents to Kyle became the foundation for him to become a loving husband and father. They stepped in and filled a void, giving him a chance in life. My hat is off to them.

Kyle somehow knew he had to make those tough choices to change the direction of his life. He had no idea that he would eventually be raised by someone who would love him so much, the way his uncle and aunt did. They gave him his own room – a place to call home during those teenage years – and they provided security for him. In Kyle's case, it made all the difference in the world. He now provides for his own wife and four sons, he has a wonderful home, he is a great husband and father. His uncle set the standard for how a man should act in the world, and how he should treat his wife. I am honored that Kyle would share his life with us all.

Kyle's story has also taught us that good people will rise up to care for a child. I have found that good-hearted adults care what happens to children, even when they are not related.

When a child has lost the fabric of their family, our hearts are torn – some more than others. One thing that's certain is that we must focus on the outcome of the guardian child's life. Thankfully, in Kyle's case, the outcome was a positive one. He'd had a turbulent time as a child, but he came through with solid values, which have stayed within him. Kyle's uncle taught him the things he needed in becoming the man he is today. He had a chance to thrive, play sports and finish growing up. This all took place during the formative years of his life, the years which would weave the very fabric of who Kyle is today. No matter what the guardian child does after your guardianship is over, the important thing is that you rose to the occasion to make a difference. Hearing from an adult child who has been raised in guardianship is a great privilege for me, especially when they have survived many tough choices.

Chapter Recap

We guardians are not the only ones making tough decisions. Some of the young children in our care are making tough decisions themselves, in the silence of their own minds. Children are looking to survive the huge shift they are in, and seeking solutions to the problems they face can be all-consuming for them. It can be overwhelming for them to adjust even to a *good* situation – as some can have a hard time accepting good things into their lives. They have become accustomed to the problems that life dishes out, and it can be just as taxing for them to get used to a new and wonderful environment. Guardians, I urge you to take the time to see if your child needs some help in processing decisions. Some of these you may have simply taken for granted, so you may need to look deeper. You're doing awesome work in making a difference for your guardian child – and the child needs you. Make the move to open the conversation with them, and see how you might help.

Section Three

When the Shift Gets Real

In this section of "When the Shift Gets Real," I will address some of the tough emotions that many of us deal with. You may feel like abandoning your new world and going back to what life was before. Hang in there! *Guardian Shift* is going to try to help you regain your sanity. Also, since those wild feelings of lost control in your life may be drowning you, you'll find a life preserver just ahead as you dive into this section. We're also going to check in with Hollywood, to see if we can glean any insights from shows they have produced. We all know that television and movies have shaped many of our perceptions. Some of these are very positive. We will see some of the ways that Hollywood portrayed life in guardianship. Of course, when things get really tough – and then, triumphantly, you prevail – this is when family is created. A special family shares their story of how their family grew by two in the midst of some difficult trials. The shift was all too real, and they will encourage you from top to bottom. This section just simply gets real, and it offers perspective in keeping everything on track. Shift on!

Chapter Twenty

Lost Relationships

This is a difficult subject. Most of us are so busy caring for the children in our newfound charge of guardianship that we don't take care of ourselves. We may have forgotten what our relationships looked like long ago. You have been in the battle of protecting children, and this has been your first and foremost objective. Rightly so! You may have had to go up against son or daughter, brother or sister, because of bad choices they entered into. Some of you have lost them to death or mental illness. Any one of these possibilities is so very sad, to say the least. Your loss of what your relationships were like before you stood up to protect the next generation needs to be addressed. They have changed – and life has moved forward. Acknowledging your heartache and working through it now becomes the goal. This is important for healing your past, smoothing out your present – and moving forward with your future. You so deserve the needed healing, and the benefits that it will bring to your family life, today and tomorrow.

Sudden Event

If you have lost a son, daughter, brother or sister to death, you're surrounded with painful memories. Whether it was caused by an illness or accident, or an abusive act, you may or may not have had an opportunity to grieve. This is a loss that many readers can identify with, though I personally have not walked in your shoes. What I do want to impart to you is that if you have not fully dealt with this loss, I want you to find a way to do so. Your loss is painful, and it simply cannot be reversed. I want to express my deepest sympathy to you. This pain does not go away, and it has to be managed. If your loss occurred by natural means, everyone feels your pain. In this case, you probably won't have the potential resentment of a loss caused by a poor set of choices.

We cannot take responsibility for the poor actions of others, but we can choose how we allow them to affect us.

I can only ask you to look into the matter and see what level of pain you are dealing with. Please seek the help of a professional counselor, pastor or trusted friend. Don't feel bad or guilty – you may have just realized that you have not dealt with this pain as well as you thought you had. For some of us, it's all a matter of timing. Issues pop into our minds at various times; we just have to find a way to work through them as they do. If you don't address these issues, they could create a barrier in the way you parent. The children who are now entrusted to your care in guardianship need you to be whole. As I mentioned earlier, "The better the lives of guardians, the better the children's lives are in guardianship."

This is the key to the whole picture – you have to have the best care for yourself in order to move forward in doing the best possible job for these little ones.

Poor Choices

When a son or daughter, brother or sister has made poor choices affecting the future, it can be maddening. These poor choices have altered the lives of their children forever – along with changing the course of life for the adults who stepped up to protect those children. This is a time where being angry can simply feel so justifiable. It can be an everyday occurrence of charged emotions. Anger on your part can fuel the fire to protect and do the right thing by the child, which is good. You may feel this anger at their choices regarding drugs, alcohol or any other form of abuse the bio-parent(s) inflicted upon the child. I know from personal experience, however, how this anger just keeps giving and giving. This is really unhealthy – and it can reach a point where you are the one left hurting, and no one else cares.

Something very odd can begin to take shape when the smoke on your battlefield begins to clear up. Your thoughts drift back to the time when things were really great between you and the son, daughter, brother or sister – and then, all of a sudden, you miss what was once a great relationship. Some of you may be able to say, "How I miss when times were good." You may be missing the son or daughter, brother or sister with whom you once shared a loving relationship. You remember how those family gatherings and childhood memories were so wonderful, and you looked upon them fondly – but now they are destroyed. If this is any part of your past, you know exactly what I am saying. You miss the times when you could hold a civil conversation, eat a meal together, and have fun with each other. Now all of that is gone! Their poor choices have caused your relationship to take a different form entirely.

I was prompted by my wife, Jeannie, to include this chapter. She has felt this loss in a highly personal way with her brother. They were very close growing up, until a couple of years after their parents divorce, when she and her brother eventually went in different directions. Later, the party scene seduced her brother, which ignited a long string of poor choices, causing separation and life-altering outcomes for us all.

Jeannie will share it from her perspective, recalling the memories from a deep and personal position. She wanted to write this to encourage you:

When my brother and I were very young, we were very close. He is only eighteen months older, and my only sibling. We always had fun together as kids, like best friends. He was protective over me as his little sister. He even took the blame sometimes when I was the one who had done something wrong. I looked up to him. He was a great big brother. Everyone knew we were close. Our parents divorced when we were nine and eleven. We managed okay, as we remained close to each other through it all. We lived with our dad (he was awarded custody), and our mom moved to another town. We saw her every other weekend and of course, on holidays, plus six weeks in the summer. Then one summer, my brother spent most of his time at our mom's house.

190

One day he called me while I was staying at my cousin's house. What he said broke my heart, and forever changed our relationship. He told me he was not coming back to live at our dad's house

> I had to come to the realization that all I could do was pray that he would turn his life around.
> —*Jeannie Amaral, guardian parent*

By this time we were teenagers, and I was about to start high school. He, meanwhile, got involved with the wrong kids and the wrong activities, and our mom had little control. I still went there on the weekends, but I didn't see him much.

I have never stopped loving my brother, and I've never stopped praying for him. His life eventually spiraled out of control with drug abuse. There were many years when I had basically "lost" my brother. Sure, I knew where he was – still living at Mom's house – but he was not the same brother I'd grown up with. Most of you know how drugs change people, and everything around them. This can cause you to feel a type of loss or grief for what used to be.

My heart hurt to see him so messed up, and not caring about making a real life for himself. There were many years during which I was just sad for him. I had to come to the realization that all I could do was pray that he would turn his life around. He was up and down over the years, and he cleaned himself up for a couple of years here and there. I had hope. I had my family, and he had

We cannot take responsibility for the poor actions of others, but we can choose how we allow them to affect us.

some children now too, but he never married any of their mothers.

My brother's struggle with drugs did not go away. It came to a point when we had to step in and take his fourteen-year-old son to raise under guardianship. Those were some very rough years, and my relationship with my brother became even more strained. But eventually, I am happy to say, my brother cleaned up his life. He got involved with a church and found Jesus. He is staying clean, and he actually got married – at age fifty. I can't tell you how good it is to talk to him on the phone, and hear him speak in a crisp, clear voice! When he was in his addiction, he would speak fast and slur his words, and it was hard to understand him. I do thank God for getting my brother's life back on track. We lost a lot of years and had a lot of heartache – and I am so thankful that he has found a life of peace. He has many regrets, and maybe some denial as to how bad his life was. But one thing is certain: there is power in prayer. Never give up! Keep praying for that brother, sister, son or daughter. There is hope! There is a bond between siblings, and between parent and child, which can't be explained away. Even though there is pain and hurt, the love never goes away!

Chapter Recap

Many of you have experienced great loss. Moving forward in life is painful if we don't reach out and get help with our pain. I hope you do! Lost relationships with a loved one are truly painful, and not to be taken lightly. Whether the loss comes from illness, sudden death or poor choices, all lead to pain. Hopefully, you gleaned something positive from Jeannie's story here. She persevered for years with the broken pieces of her family. It was painful to see and feel her pain, but she is strong. As a family, we did what our hearts told us to do – to protect a young boy, at all costs!

We thought that our family would be supportive of our role – but many of them wanted to tell us how to do it. Their skewed thinking led us to exercise our own role as guardians, and let them know we were in charge. This caused the loss of relationships, but we did what was right. We cannot take responsibility for the poor actions of others, but we can choose how we allow them to affect us. Sometimes a lost relationship will come back around, and this is what we hope for. Forge on – as the Shift changes lives in a way we never see coming!

Chapter Twenty-One

Can I Get a Redo?

Some of you might love having a redo of your guardianship life. Let's clear up the feelings of guilt that you may be feeling. It's okay. We know we did the right thing to protect the child in our care, but no one prepared us for this role. I want to define "redo" as it relates to this emotion that some of you may be feeling, along with thoughts like "I would love to go back in time, and perhaps choose a different path." I will relate this emotion to the child playing a game and asking for a "do-over." It's not as if we took a class in school for this chapter of our lives. For that matter, many of us who have concluded our guardianships may *still* feel as if we want a redo! My wife and I have often felt this way, years after we were finished raising our nephew, although it is the very fuel that brings me to writing this book. It is truly our goal to help alleviate any possible regrets.

As you already know, and as I've mentioned repeatedly, guardianship has changed the direction of your life. We are all the result of our life experiences. The painful thing I am writing now is that if you give up on parenting in guardianship, you will always have this experience within you – and you will also have the experience of giving up. I doubt that you want to experience the thought of "what if I had only continued on?" The bravery you need to make it through this time in life comes from the fact that time passes quickly – believe it or not – and you *will* get through this! This role requires tenacity, and it's a role that can define your character in many ways. Are you committed? Are you dependable, caring, loving? The list goes on. Guardianship can develop you into a person you never thought you could ever be! Think back to Emily, the nineteen-year-old from England, who took in her niece and nephew – and who experienced personal growth beyond imagination.

> *It's not as if we took a class in school for this chapter of our lives.*

You may be a guardian, but I am confident that you aren't doing this because you're seeking respect. You may not *be* respected or appreciated, and it's disappointing. Your guardian child or the extended family members may *not* respect you. All you can think of is what you're doing for them – and they have *no clue!* But consider the source… they don't have the child themselves, because they *are* clueless. You should not look to derive your worth from the ones who are disrespecting you. They are the *last* people you are going to get respect from. Respect will come from those who understand your journey of guardianship. This is why it's so important to connect with others who understand what it's like to raise other people's children. This is the main reason why I have created a private Facebook group that's strictly for guardians and their support people (see Section Six for connection details).

The ones who stood by you and have remained by your side are your cheerleaders. Let's filter out all the adults who seem to have put you in this role, because who would want the respect of those who endangered the child in your care? You will always have your "Haters Fan Club," and well... you are just going to have to let them hate. It's *their* problem. You can't control them. One day they may come to some sort of clarity. This leaves the rest of the people in your life, but even they still need some sorting. You have those who smile and say nice things to you, but who look smugly down their nose at you for bringing this disrupting lifestyle upon yourself. For example, I met a family from the East Coast who took three children into their home as foster children. Once their close friends became fully aware of this undertaking, they basically turned their backs on them. This was painful for the family, and it left them confused. They don't get it either. It may be difficult to determine who is actually on your side while you're in guardianship – or then again, it may be very obvious.

The real group of trustworthy supporters in your inner circle may be rather limited. You might even have more fingers on one hand than you have people in your inner circle. If so, I am writing to *you*. But, let me assure you, there can be plenty of joy during this time of feeling isolated and alone. These inner-circle people for

You will always have your "Haters Fan Club," and well... you are just going to have to let them hate. It's their problem.

197

Jeannie and me were the ones who carried us through the battle of obtaining guardianship, through our life with our nephew, and to our guardianship's conclusion. Many people in your life may not be supportive because they just don't know how to be. As you think about those who are encouraging to you, I am hoping you are feeling thankful for them. These are your support people. Though some of them may surprise you as to who they are, be sure to show them how much you appreciate them. It could be someone you met in court who stays with you for the rest of your journey. It could be an old friend who you just reconnected with. But the main point is that they have become your inner circle – and this is all that matters.

Your inner circle is what helps you maintain your sanity in the middle of wanting a redo in your role as a guardian. They are the ones who will help you remember why you stepped in to protect this child in the first place. They will hold your hand when all you can do is cry because your entire family is out of balance. Things have become chaotic as you have had to do battle on all fronts. No one seems to understand the fact that you had to sacrifice so much to protect your guardian child. Often the bio-parent is off running around with their friends, if they are not incarcerated. You see them living it up on Facebook, and your feelings of frustration arise. But don't get distracted by them. Believe me, for your own sanity, you need to organize your thinking around what is best for your guardian child. Stay focused. For those bio-parents who are somewhat functional and appear to be having

Find those shoulders you can cry on, and move forward toward your goal of raising a healthy, well-balanced child in guardianship.

a good time, don't be envious of their life. The roles have all shifted, and you need to know each person's role in this new family paradigm you're in now. Remember what guardians do? "Guardians *guard*" – and that is our role. Hold on to that concept. Don't allow the bio-parent to have any control over your emotions or feelings. If so, negative thoughts might interfere with the important job you are doing.

Chapter Recap

As we peer into our emotions of wanting a redo, remember that this is normal. Let's not be ashamed that we may want things to be the way they used to be. It's a natural and justifiable emotion. We just need to remember the title we hold – and that is the title of Guardian. This is what we do. Your whole world just shifted at the core of your life. You're entitled to your feelings – your pain is real. But course corrections in your thinking will resolve this taunting emotion. A redo of your guardianship would rock the world of the child in your care. Stay strong! Find those shoulders you can cry on, and move forward toward your goal of raising a healthy, well-balanced child in guardianship.

Chapter Twenty-Two

Out of Balance?

Since some of you may find yourselves out of balance, let's take a look at making some adjustments. It may only be in certain areas of your life, versus "My whole life is out of whack," which some of you may be thinking. This can cause a lot of stress, depending on which areas of your life are out of balance. In our hearts we may already know which areas those are. Perhaps they're your relationships with your spouse, your children, your close friends. Discovering other areas may take some soul searching. When any area is affected, whether it's work, staying organized, spiritual nurturing, recreation, rest, exercise, friendships, or anything else that you value, you will start to suffer emotionally, physically and mentally, and you can become overwhelmed.

Being out of balance takes many forms. It may start with all of your energy raging, in a focused attempt to protect the

If you were someone who spent time and energy in the war to protect, you're the one I am concerned with right now. You're the one who feels like a bicycle with bent spokes.

child from the environment they were in. You may have spent months or even years in this mode, which could have left you way out of balance. If you were someone who spent time and energy in the war to protect, you're the one I am concerned with right now. You're the one who feels like a bicycle with bent spokes. During this time that you spent protecting, you most likely neglected other areas of your life. For those of you who have a spouse and children of your own, you may have left some damage in the wake of your quest. Although it was a noble task that you were undertaking, I personally believe you never once intended to hurt anyone in your quest to protect. It just happened. Rebalancing can have its challenges as you attempt to align your life and reset your priorities. Some of those you neglected could be a bit bent out of shape too. They are entitled to their feelings – even though they may have been supportive early on, and then turned that support to silent angst. The good news is that if you keep your cool while working out your rebalancing act, it will work out. The motto "Stay calm and carry on" is excellent advice from the Brits.

With those you love, of course, these are the ones out of balance with you. Hopefully, they will forgive you for this hurt later on, as they deal with it. It will take extra bravery on your part, though. This is difficult – but you will be happy you did it. Just take a deep breath, and realize that it is a privileged path for you to protect your guardian child. This should give you the right mindset to approach the conversation of rebalancing.

Please don't cop an attitude that you were on this "mission of mercy" to protect the child in your care. The best approach is to recognize the potential wounds around you, and deal with them.

Once your loved ones see that you understand how they feel, the conversation will start to flow. Just keep your cool. Your immediate family is your closest inner circle, and probably your strongest "support peeps." Let them express to you what happened along the journey to protect. I did not see it while I was on this 24-7 mission myself, and my three sons were catching the brunt of Daddy not being as available when they needed him. They were all neglected in one way or another – and I should add my wife to the neglect list as well. To all of our surprise, it took more out of *me* than we ever even knew it would. I was so out of whack that I didn't see it – and this went on for a long time.

Not going into the details of my out-of-balance journey too much, I am prepared to let you know how I regained my balance. I had to go to each one of my sons, and my wife, to discuss the family imbalance that had occurred, without letting my nephew know what was going on around him. I didn't want to allow any opportunity for guilt to come up for him, and make him feel that he was an inconvenience to us. Once I took the time to gather my thoughts on what had happened, I was able to have the right perspective in my heart to begin to heal the hurts. Each of my boys was so very supportive when I raised the topic. I wanted them to know how sorry I was

Your focus to protect a child is more important than what other people think. It is vital to find the ways to rebalance your life and create harmony once again.

that they weren't getting the attention they so deserved from me while I was investing so much time into my nephew. They understood, looking past my "imbalance infraction," and they never doubted that they were special to me. This didn't happen overnight, but once I got the ball rolling, it became evident to them that I *was* there for them. My wife and I were able to cut back on the amount of time we spent discussing the drama in our nephew's life, and the negative behavior of the people who helped him arrive into our hands. We made a commitment that we were no longer going to give all of those people any more of our lives. So my suggestion to you is not to give your life up by talking about the negative people who helped bring you to your guardianship role. Don't make the big mistake of dwelling on it. It will hurt the ones you love – and it will hurt *you*.

Addressing balance is important. Being resilient is also key for you to sustain yourself. As you practice your own balancing act, you also have to ask yourself lots of questions before you do this or that. Your new goal is to live a balanced life while developing a positive outcome for you and your family. Every time you have an intrusion from those who are negative toward you, ask yourself, "How much of my life am I going to give to this or that person?" You need to decide how much you're willing to open yourself up. Those particular people in your life will soon get the point that they can't just roll into your day and create a toxic environment. They will begin to understand that they are limited in getting *any* of your attention. Frankly, they don't deserve more

Your biological children, too, will be much happier once you have set the boundaries for those other family members.

204

than what *you say* they can have. You are in control of this new "diet" of how you spend your time. They will kick and scream a bit at first, but the new boundaries will be good for all of you. Your biological children will be much happier once you have set the boundaries for those other family members. Your spouse will be happier too, since you won't have any more long, tiring talks about the "out-laws" who put you in this role. You will begin to see balance coming back into your life. This will give you a feeling of empowerment, bringing happiness and relief as well. You'll also notice that your feelings of wanting a redo on the guardianship merry-go-round are starting to disappear. You will become a leader to those who need to be led – for example, the bio-parents and other relatives – who typically suck the life out of you.

Chapter Recap

As you seek rebalancing, you may ruffle a few feathers along the way. Managing those who feel they have the right to step into your life, and shake up your world, *will* get easier. Limit them, and help them understand the importance of balance for everybody. It may take a while before they get it. If they don't, just keep in mind that you're not here to please them – you are here to care for the next generation.

Please evaluate your family balance. If it is tipped in the wrong direction (towards neglect), you will need to spend some time bringing it back toward the center. This is key for your family – especially your children by birth– who need you as much as (or more than) your child in guardianship does. Your spouse needs you, but more importantly you truly need them, as they are the backbone to your household.

Your focus to protect a child is more important than what other people think. It is vital to find the ways to rebalance your life and create harmony once again. It's all about your health as a guardian – and the better *your* health, the better care you can provide to your entire family. That's what it's about!

Chapter Twenty-Three

Hollywood and Beyond

Raising other people's children is as old as time, it seems. We see it back in Bible times with the story of Esther, the queen who was raised by her cousin Mordecai.[1] For the 2006 movie, "One Night with the King,"[2] about this story, Mordecai was referred to as Esther's "Foster-Dad," in an article.[3] People have been raising other people's children for a very long time, although it may be new to you or me in our own lives.

When our boys were young, we watched all the action-adventure movies, but not many princess or girly films. But, once the boys were all grown up and our daughter was now the one watching movies with us, that all changed. At one point, when we were disgusted with what was available on TV, we started checking out DVDs at the local library on a regular basis, keeping in mind that we were looking for movies our daughter would enjoy. After a dozen-plus hours of Shirley

Perhaps this powerful scene from Fresh Prince of Bel-Air will give you a glimpse of the immense pain in a child's heart when they are hurt by a selfish parent.

Temple movies, I thought that we must have watched every one ever made. Not true! They were good, wholesome, cute and sweet. Yes, this about sums up those movies – but you know, after a while, we noticed a similar thread in most of the Shirley Temple films. She was almost always an orphan (adorable, I might add)! She was either being raised by her grandfather (in "Heidi"[4]) or an aunt (in "Rebecca of Sunnybrook Farm"[5]) or even some unrelated people (in "Bright Eyes"[6]). These movies were made back in the 1930s – so it is not a new story line at all!

The Fresh Prince of Bel-Air

Many of you may have watched the '90s television show "The Fresh Prince of Bel-Air."[7] The show portrays Will Smith as the nephew from the East Coast who'd had some rough times growing up alone, without much parental supervision. Then his uncle and aunt, in the affluent Bel-Air neighborhood of Southern California, took Will in. This makes for a completely different lifestyle for both Will and the new guardian family, which makes the show fun. But there are some serious points. Will brought a certain flair of excitement, even though two worlds collided in SoCal. You could feel the love from his new family, wanting him to feel secure and to help him. Interactions often were awkward between the siblings, but they always looked after one another.

The greatest scene of the entire show was when Will's dad was going to take him on a father-son camping trip. You can find the clip online.[8] Search for the "Greatest Scene of The Fresh Prince of Bel-Air" – it is about three minutes in length. It cuts in where Will's dad is telling Will's uncle that he can't take Will on the camping trip. Uncle Phil says he won't do Daddy's dirty work of telling Will the disappointing news, just as Daddy is cutting out and Will comes into the room, packed and ready to head out with his dad. Dad turns back into the room to tell Will that he had some business come up, and can't make it. From this point on, I want you to go to YouTube to see it – it is worth watching. I have heard that what happens next was not scripted at all. I am not completely sure of this, but you can feel the power of pure, raw emotion. Have some tissues handy, because it will bring tears to your eyes. Your soul will hurt for Will. Perhaps this powerful scene from Fresh Prince of Bel-Air will give you a glimpse of the immense pain in a child's heart when they are hurt by a selfish parent.

It is just all too common for the bio-parents to hurt the child in your care. Children so want to be loved by their parents, and to make them proud. I wish there was a way to curb this, but I think it is in every child's DNA. Many of you, I am sure, have had these run-ins with the bio-parents, and it's never easy. As I've mentioned several times in this book, guardians are guards – and this reminder will create the fuel for you to make sure that the bio-parents' hurtful nature is controlled or limited. This is what's best for the child. It's also the best for your own mental well-being.

We only get one day at a time, and what we do with today will improve our tomorrow.

Ruby & the Rockits

Another TV show, which aired in the fall of 2009 on ABC, was "Ruby & the Rockits,"[9] starring David Cassidy and Alexa PenaVega as father and daughter. Alexa plays Ruby Gallagher, whose mother died when she was twelve. She moves in with her grandparents, who she claims forgot she was even there, so she goes to find her dad. David, the dad, is not so excited to meet her, and he feels she will cramp his rock-star lifestyle. So he goes to his brother (played by his real-life half-brother, Patrick Cassidy), and his wife, who are raising two sons of their own, to ask for help with Ruby. Uncle Patrick and Aunt Audie take her in and make her feel like part of their family. The whole "family" thing is new to her, but she seems to like it and does well with the adjustments. You can watch some clips from this show, too, on YouTube. We thought it was a great show, and it's another example of a shift in guardians as shown on TV. Her dad was still involved in her life to some degree, which was complicated by tension between him and his brother. "Ruby and the Rockits" succeeded in portraying the need for love and stability in this young girl's life, all the while bringing humor and light-heartedness to the story.

We were disappointed that the show was cancelled after only one season, not only because we enjoyed it, but because we are blessed to personally know Alexa PenaVega. We met her and her family several years ago, when they were on vacation. We have enjoyed watching her grow up and become a great woman of faith, and see her stand up for it in Hollywood. Young leaders like Alexa and her husband Carlos (who were recently on 'Dancing With The Stars' Season 21) are trend setters, bringing values back into the filmmaking industry. They show the children in our care that it is cool to love God and make good choices. "Ruby and the Rockits" will always be part of my memories, as it related to real-world guardianship and the responsibility that you and I have had to carry out, on behalf of those who could not.

The Beverly Hillbillies

Now I am going to date myself a bit here. I remember watching the "The Beverly Hillbillies"[9] as a child. You may recall (it's okay to sing this part!) *"...It's a story about a man named Jed, who barely kept his family fed. Then one day, out shooting for some food, then up from the ground came a-bubbling crude. (Oil, that is. Black gold...)."* The next thing you know, Jed is packing up the car with his daughter, mother-in-law and nephew. I am not clear in my memory on how Jethro, the nephew, came to live with them. However, Jethro was loved and cared for well as the show goes on – having money and super toys, as any young man in Beverly Hills would have – except with one twist. All his ways were always intertwined with his hillbilly ways – and this is what made the show so entertaining. Jethro and Elly May, Jed's daughter, were always getting up to some sort of adventure at the mansion. Granny was always toting around her shotgun for protection. She scared off plenty of salesmen from the front door, but Jed always seemed to find a way to spend some money on whatever they were selling. Jethro loved his uncle, and he and Elly May were always bird-dogging a wife for Pa. My best memories are of the tight family bond that always showed up in every episode. They were a family, kind of crazy at times, but they stuck together.

Those of us starring in our own show of guardian life can learn a bit of wisdom from these TV programs. We can love those in our care, and help them remember that if they put a little thought into scripting their life, it may turn out to be a fun adventure. So let's look for the ways we can script a little fun and adventure into our guardianship worlds. It's a fact that life is happening whether we plan it or not, so why not plan it out. You can start today to make the plan – and don't ever think you are too far into life to develop one. We only get one day at a time, and what we do with today will improve our tomorrow. So kick it into gear, get out your notebook (or laptop), and outline how you want it to look – then create an action plan to get there.

Scripting

Writing out goals is really useful. Writing out the script of your life is something that will stimulate your mind. This gives you clarity of the direction you want to go. Just think – you're the one doing the writing, and you're free to write it any way you want. One important note: you must write it from the heart, and not from a "wish list." Writing a script of your future life is powerful, so be honest with yourself in your design. You will feel it as you write it out. I did this myself, in early 2015 – I simply got in touch with the areas of my life that were most important to me. Finishing this book – as well as the others I have planned to follow it in this series – is key to that script. I know, because I wrote out this book as part of my script, and it has come to life for me, with the

Writing a script of your future life is powerful, so be honest with yourself in your design.

main goal of encouraging you. I have other personal areas of my life in my script as well. I collaborated with Jeannie, so that we would both be on the same page while pursuing the plan. The last thing I wanted was not to be of the same mind as Jeannie. She helped me focus the script, which was especially valuable because we would both be affected by my following it. You can start by just jotting down what is important to you, and then building from that. Scratch off those items that may not be part of the direction you really want to go. Best of all, have fun with it!

Today

Getting started today is key – waiting will never produce a different result in your life! You will be glad you took the time. It's simply never too late to start to script your life. If we just let life happen without planning well, we will receive whatever life wants to give us – and this may not be our preferred outcome. I recommend doing something about it. Getting started will begin to get our minds thinking, and this leads to a changed future. I am no expert in this area, and there are plenty of good books on this subject by those who *are* experts. Search online for leaders in the area of planning your life, and read up. Many of them are so helpful in showing you how to go about this. Treat yourself to planning and scripting, and then you can begin to set an action plan in motion for each area of your new plan. I used pictures in my plan to bring more clarity to my written statements. You may consider this too. Mix it up and get as creative as possible. The power of visual aids can bring it to life. Once again, have fun with it!

Chapter Recap

It's no secret that Hollywood has shaped the perceptions of people around the world. For us, it was often positive and very educational to watch Hollywood portray guardianship. They put careful planning into the programs they aired to give us good family fun. So why wouldn't you put some thought and time into designing the program of your own life? As you look at planning, remember that you deserve to have a vision of the days ahead of you. Just think, if one thing that you script comes together for you, how great would it feel? It could be very encouraging! Having a good plan – an outline of your life – could impact you and your guardian child beyond measure. We all have parts of our lives that we want to change. In fact, you are changing the life of the child in your care, right? You intuitively did this – now it's time to be acting with purpose. Plan a life of your design, be true to your heart – and go for it!

Chapter Twenty-Four

DNA… Family?

Some of the best opportunities to learn come from hearing someone else's story. I have heard many of them during the last several years of putting this book together. The one you are about to read is both moving and encouraging. I recently had the pleasure of meeting Chris, I asked him if he would share his story to encourage us. He agreed, but he found himself in some dark memories at times while putting it together for you and me. You will fall in love with this precious family. The trials and the waiting were painful for them, but so well worth it. While visiting with them, I found this couple to have huge hearts of compassion.

Please saddle up with a box of tissues handy, and enjoy what's to come as Chris takes us through his families life-changing journey. In his own words, written with you in mind, he offers to encourage you. Chris wants you to continue running the race of your personal journey!

Life has an uncanny way of being something we never pictured it to be. Without any warning, it has the ability to turn everything we know and believe on its head – leaving us in a whirlwind of unanswered questions, "what-ifs" and, too often, tears. Call it karma, the luck of the draw, fate, or the intervention of the divine. But whatever you do, don't call it an accident. These moments, as horribly frightening as they are in the moment, are purposeful – and they're designed to bring out things we never knew dwelt within us.

In 2010, what I choose to believe was God's divine providence began in our family. It is a journey that has transformed each and every member of my family in ways we never dreamed possible. Looking back, I can actually say that the groundwork was being laid for this adventure long before 2010. I can see now why the events in my life that I'm about to describe took place. Because without them, two of the greatest blessings in our lives would never have arrived.

I spent nearly thirteen years in the United States Air Force. My family was happy with the military life. We loved moving to new locations, having the security of the Armed Forces, and serving our great nation. So in 2008, I was devastated to learn that I had developed asthma. For anyone familiar with the military, you'll know that asthma is typically a death sentence to a military career. My diagnosis certainly was. It began a long process, which eventually ended

> *It's amazing what a family will do to avoid facing their demons. Overnight, my family was transformed into traitors.*
> *–Chris Mathews, guardian parent*

in my discharge from the service. But as you will see later in this story, without it, our lives and the lives of two wonderful children would look extremely different.

Shortly after my wife and I married, her mother remarried. From my new father-in-law's side, two beautiful nieces would be brought into our extended family. Their lives didn't have the highest odds of turning out to be a fairy tale. I'm not saying that their parents didn't love them, or even that the parents were bad people. I know, to this day, that their parents love them with all the love they can offer. But some people can offer more than others. Please understand that this isn't an attempt to belittle the girls' parents in any way. I'm merely stating the facts – some parents are simply limited, because of the baggage they have brought into their adult lives, in being able to love their children in the way that the children deserve. These girls were brought into a family dynamic that could easily be referred to as a tinderbox pine forest, surrounded by men with flamethrowers. For a number of years, we did all we could to be a steady presence in their young lives. We often took them for weeks on end during the summers, and we did everything we could to be a voice of stability in their minds and hearts. We knew that their parents loved them; wanted the best for them even. We never for a moment doubted that if the parents could, they would give these girls the happiness they deserved and desired. We simply wanted to model to the children, and to the parents as well, what life outside of the chaos they saw each day could look like.

In 2005, we had the opportunity to relocate to San Diego, California. This move would place us within ten miles of the girls, and we jumped at the chance. The first two years were wonderful. We would visit with them regularly, have their entire family over frequently, and spend quality time with them all. We hoped and prayed that our relationship with the family would become a stabilizing force in the children's lives. We had good relationships with their parents and grandparents. We tried to be there for all of them in any circumstance or hardship they faced. But in 2007, all of that changed in one horrifying moment.

Coming home in a drunken rage one evening, their father drew a gun on their mother, in plain sight of both girls. He then chambered a round and told his wife, "This bullet is for you," as he placed the barrel on her temple. By the grace of God another family member was able to intervene and stop him from pulling the trigger, but the hatred in his heart had found its mark. That evening every good intention, every attempt to be what the children needed, every heartfelt desire to love them with unbridled passion melted in the flames of hatred and jealousy. Their father would never again occupy a safe place in the girls' hearts or minds. He could never again be trusted with the trust that only a child can have – and no words or actions could ever change that.

To make matters worse for the girls, their mother had lived in this cycle of abuse for many years. Her reaction to this episode would be no different than any of the others, returning to and even defending her abuser. She made excuses for his behavior, and her fear of being alone outweighed her desire to give her children a safe haven, free from this form of violence. In a few short weeks we found that she was violating the court orders that prevented him from any contact with the children, and had moved back in with him. For us, it was the final straw in a long series of backbreakers.

Little did we know that these six months would become a permanent, and life-changing arrangement for all of us.
–Chris Mathews, guardian parent

Believing we had no other option for the safety of the children, we called the police and informed them of the violation. Their father was subsequently arrested, and we were permanently shut out of their lives. It's amazing what a family will do to avoid facing their demons. Overnight, my family was transformed into traitors. Both sides of the family came against us in full force, accusing us of wrecking their home and taking the girls' father away from them. They all circled the wagons, unwilling to look at the events as a wake-up call, but chose instead to use our actions to justify staying together. They were suddenly the victims, and they could now join together to fight their common enemy. We quickly withdrew, but the lessons we learned in this little episode were merely a small taste of what would come our way three years later.

In November of 2010, after three years of no contact with the girls or their parents, we received a phone *call that changed our lives forever. At this point, I had been discharged from the military and had moved alone to Santa Maria, California, over seven hours away. I was there testing the waters of a new career before I brought my wife and children to join me. We had decided that moving to Santa Maria was the best plan for our family, and we intended to move everyone during the Christmas break. I was working there that Thanksgiving, while my wife was spending it with her mother in San Diego. I had come to my car to check my messages, and found one from my wife, saying that state child welfare services would be removing the children from their mother's care the next day.*

The girls and their parents had completely fallen off the radar for three years. No one in the family knew anything of their whereabouts, or what condition they were in. Apparently, the situation had become far worse than anyone could have imagined. With state social services ready to step in, their mother was looking feverishly for a place to send the girls. Sadly, no immediate relatives were willing to take both girls together. In the last three years, the only stability the girls had known was what they found in each other. They each knew that regardless of the situation, the other would always be there. My wife and I decided we had to at least offer to take both girls, regardless of how the family viewed us.

Our story can be summed up in this way – a simple act can forever change a life. It isn't about where the children in this story came from. It's all about where they will end up.
–Chris Mathews, guardian parent

On November 30th, 2010, we pulled up to the trailer the girls had been living in. We arrived to a darkened trailer, devoid of electricity, with the girls and their mother standing in the driveway awaiting our arrival. As the girls were getting into the car, their mother handed us a small box that contained all their earthly possessions. Everyone said their goodbyes, and we drove away to begin what would become one of the most challenging years of our marriage. We had agreed to six months of custody, to allow the children's mother the opportunity to rearrange her life, and afterwards, to give the girls the life they deserved. Little did we know that these six months would become a permanent, and life-changing arrangement for all of us.

This story will not delve into the depth of depravity that our "daughters" had endured. There is no need to describe the heart-wrenching and deplorable details that led to their filling a place in our lives forever. Anyone who has been asked to do what our family did on that day undoubtedly knows already that the details are cruel and unfair, and that they bring pain to our hearts that we simply cannot endure at times. Our story isn't about the details that brought the girls into our care. Instead, our story can be summed up in this way – a simple act can forever change a life. It isn't about where the children in this story came from. It's all about where they will end up.

When I look back on all the small events that enabled my family to be exactly where we were, at exactly the moment we needed to be – which gave us the courage to try, and the will to fight – I can say with all confidence that God orchestrated each and every step of our lives. When I look at the lives that our girls are leading now, and the change in my family because of their presence, I can say without a doubt that God has a purpose for them that is far greater than they could ever imagine. There are a million ways my life could be different right now. There are a thousand paths that each of us can walk, and sometimes we all look back and say, "If I'd only stepped in the other direction." One of the greatest lessons I've learned through all of this is that whatever path I'm standing on, it's exactly the path God intended me to be on. Every event in my life – every choice I have made, every misstep and miscue, each and every tick of life's clock – led me (and each member of my family) directly to the place where two little girls would need someone to love them.

It is extremely likely that you've had doubts, or require encouragement, about whatever decision you've made that led you to be reading this book in the first place. The struggles of raising a child who is not your own are many, and they bring with them headaches and heartaches that only a small percentage of people in this world could ever begin to comprehend. There are the families who make us the villains. The children who adore the parents who abused them. The outbursts and the tears. The infinite list of items that people in our positions have to contend with. But there is one thing that I am certain of – we were meant to contend with it.

Each of us reading this book was placed on this Earth at this time for a purpose. In all likelihood, this purpose is the child(ren) to whom you opened your heart and your home. Think about it! Really, truly, ponder that for a moment. It's easy to overlook the impact of the decision to open your lives to a child in need. It's easy to be bogged down with the negatives in their stories. When we are faced with the constant stress and strain of raising a child from a relative's home, we can far too easily be sucked into the vortex of destruction that brought them to our doorstep. It's easy for us to say, "If I had only (fill in the blank), my life wouldn't have taken this turn." We wouldn't have the sleepless nights, the tears of rejection, the broken hearts when the courts decide that the bio-parents are trying "hard enough." But, if you hadn't been exactly where you were in your journey of life, those children wouldn't have any hope. You, I, we – are that hope.

Our girls definitely struggled after they came to live with us. For the next two years we saw them removed from our home, shuttled around from parent to parent again, and eventually sent back to us. We held them when the night terrors woke them from their sleep. We cried with them when they came to realize exactly who their parents were. We struggled with them as they fought to overcome the demons they were dealing with from the past they endured. In short, we loved them. Love isn't just that warm feeling in the pit of our stomach or the tingle we get down our spine. Love is devotion to someone, even when that someone requires us to share *in their pain. Raising any child requires this kind of love. Raising one who isn't your own requires it even more.*

I don't want to give the impression that we have something that others do not. I assure you, we aren't special. We have the same struggles and insecurities that everyone shares. If you are questioning your ability to do this, I want our story to let you know that YOU CAN DO THIS!!!! Your life, your story, everything you've ever done has led you to this place at this time. You have everything you need to make it through to the other side – and when you do, you will be amazed at the person you have become and the person you have raised.

Our story isn't finished yet. We have had our girls for five years, and they are now teenagers. We were awarded permanent custody in 2012, and we have done everything in our power to raise the girls as if they are our own two children. They are the most beautiful young ladies I have ever met. One is passionate for children and for missions. She devotes much of her spare time to volunteering with kids at church, and she hopes to be a missionary when she graduates high school. The other has a passion for life that is unmatched. She can light up a room with her laughter, and loves just about any sport she can play. The transformation in them both has been nothing short of a miracle. When the girls first arrived at our home, they slept for three days. Literally, three days! One's nerves were so shot that she shook almost continuously for two years. One couldn't read or write at a first-grade level, and she was in third grade. The defeated and broken children who arrived at our door have become victorious. They overcame the worst odds that any child could be born into – and made themselves into champions.

As I said at the beginning of our story, life has an uncanny way of becoming something we never pictured it to be. Five years ago, I never would have dreamed I'd be sitting here writing this story to be included in a book. Three years ago, I was wondering what in the world I had done that had led me to the pain my family was going through. You may be in a similar situation today. The best advice I could offer you is to embrace each and every surprise that this life of ours throws your way. This life we have is full of surprises – and two of the best surprises it's ever thrown at me now call me "Dad"!

Chapter Recap

Maybe you're wiping some tears at this point? I hope you are as moved and encouraged as I am. I know Chris poured his heart and soul out as he shared his story. They were meant to be a family, and now they are whole. The girls are doing great now, and they have adjusted very well to life. The whole family has integrated very well. I have to say that I wish I could have had the opportunity to hear of stories like this when Jeannie and I were in the midst of our own guardianship. This kept our fire burning to get Guardian Shift written and into your hands. Just because someone is not related to you doesn't mean you can't call them family. Love for a child crosses all boundaries – geography, ethnicity and DNA. It's our love that matters, as love is the greatest binder of all in creating family.

Section Four

Shifting Boldly into the Future

In this section, I take you on a journey of looking forward. It will bring you some insights for your future planning. "Shifting Boldly into the Future" is all about working on matters in which your future points of view are created and clarified. *Guardian Shift* helps you create goals and values that you design for your family. I will assist you in learning what language your guardian child speaks, and how best to show love to them. You will become a firm believer in writing down those things that are on your mind. Journaling will be a part of this section. While reading through the following chapters, you will see how you can find the time to add journaling to your schedule, while reaping the benefits of doing this. Some of my favorite topics lie ahead, such as making better choices, and casting an eye towards finishing well. This section, "Shifting Boldly into the Future," will give you tools to enhance your guardianship journey. You will find my offer to connect right after this section. Please take me up on it.

Chapter Twenty-Five

Values

The subject of family values is a bit complicated as it relates to families of guardianship. You have already created your values before you brought the grandchild, niece or nephew into your family. Depending on the age of the child in your guardianship care, they have already come with some preprogramming of their own. Let's face it, though, in most cases they wouldn't be in your care if that programming didn't already have some faulty wiring. You have lived a lifetime of being set in the direction you've chosen to go, as a leader in your home. Now you have someone new to integrate, and to try to balance to your core values. In today's world, you can write out your family values much as you would a business plan. My middle son Spencer asked me one time, while I was in the seventh year of putting this book series together, "Dad, what's the plan?" I paused long and hard. I said "It's to bring love to as many families of guardianship as I possibly can – and that's it!" Things grew in a very positive way from that moment forward. I continued to ask myself the tough questions, such as "How am I going to do this?" "What do guardians need to improve their lives at this moment?" and "How will I pull this all together?" I always knew what I wanted to convey, but a written plan brings clarity.

I created a list of important values that would be required to bring this project to life. I then focused on the most important values first, with the objective to serve you in the best way possible. You were always on my mind as I feverishly worked on "The Plan." When you commit things to paper (or the digital equivalent!), they seem to take on a life of their own. This is very much like goal setting. Once I arrived at the most important items to include in the plan, I began to write out a description of exactly what each one would look like. This set the foundation for me to show my overview to my wife Jeannie for her review and critiquing. Jeannie kept me accountable to stay on track, without running off on a tangent. The plan was designed to be the most beneficial that it could be. Jeannie was involved – from concept to completion – when I decided to write **Guardian Shift**. Together we set milestones, and we established the tone for this book. When it came down to image, website and publishing style, we gathered a team of designers, editors and publishing consultants to guide us.

Knowing that each of you are finding your own set of values to better your family is a powerful step in building your guardian child's life.

How does this relate to family values? It involves many of the attributes of setting up your personal family value system. You have to establish what is important to you, and then how you will impart that to your existing family and to the new child in your care. Once you have reached your goal, the execution may become an entirely new issue. Your biological children will most likely be fine about the situation as you approach the subject, but your guardian child might say, "Hey, this is way off from where my thinking is." They may not say it just like that, but they could leave you thinking that this is what they meant by their reaction to your new philosophy. You will have your work cut out for you in gently establishing the belief structure that will ultimately set a new course for your guardian child.

As you explore the process of creating family values, be sure to add in the most salient points. Here is a short list to start with: social aspects, religion, work, morals and recreation. This is in no way an all-inclusive list; it's just a framework. We were a family who put God first in our lives, and not all of you may agree on this. We put Him at the top of our list. It was important to us that our children and our nephew had a solid foundation in this regard. For us, once this first building block was placed, it set the tone for all the others. It helped all of our children to do their studies, to the best of their capabilities, and to push harder, while looking to God for direction. However you decide to lay your own foundation of family values, seek out a solid foundation that will complement what you want to impart to your children for a lifetime. Knowing that each of you are finding your own set of values to better your family is a powerful step in building your guardian child's life.

Moving forward, implementing and restructuring values with your guardian child will bring its challenges. This is a

You may have heard that no one cares what you have to say – until they all know how much you care. This is true, and this is how we all think.

hard one. Depending on their age, the drama they have been through, and their maturity level, the way you deliver these values is something that you need to plan carefully. Some children in guardianship are ready to take on a more positive lifestyle, while others are holding onto the old, damaging framework from their bio-parents. The children could even be doing this out of guilt that they may feel for allowing a new parent figure to direct their lives. This guilt won't go away on its own – you will need to talk it through to filter it out.

You're now walking a very tough road. Later in this section of the book, I speak about the importance of finishing well, with an eye on your guardian child's adulthood. I found that if I dwelled too much on the past experiences that they have been through, it's this that becomes the focus. My advice is to remind them of the love that their biological parents have for them, and assure them that their biological parents would only want what's best for them. You cannot take away the bond that they have with their parents, or the loyalty that they feel. If you do, you will become the enemy. On the other hand, once you have established the fact that you are *not* taking away their parents, the tension should ease. Now you can introduce the new concept of why these new values – *your* values – are important. I was always looking to help our nephew "raise the bar" in his decisions. My advice to you is to help your family understand the importance of establishing a strong value system into their lives – and how it could protect their future outcomes. It will help to launch them into adulthood securely – even though they may think that that day is a hundred years away!

Your family's value system should be able to tie directly into your guardian child's goals and aspirations for their lives. Once you have connected those dots, you will be able to span the timeline from today to the moment when they begin their adult life. You will focus on the path they will need to follow to get what they want, and need, out of life. Remind them that either way, if they plan, they will achieve – and if they fail to plan, they will receive whatever life hands them. It is better to plan one's own future than to just let the cards fall randomly, which could produce an undesirable outcome. Help your guardian child understand that planning is power, and that you are their cheerleader for all they do. You may have heard that no one cares what you have to say – until they *all* know how much you care. This is true, and this is how we all think. Eliminate this from the start, and you will have your guardian child's attention. You will impart your value system – and you will help them set goals to finish well.

To maintain these values, you may have to revisit them often. I recommend sitting down with your values once a week for a few minutes, and allow modifications and conversation to flow. Your children will love to talk about themselves, now and in the future. They will enjoy talking about the lives they will be leading, and the people they will become. Hopes and dreams will flow from these

> *Remind them that either way, if they plan, they will achieve – and if they fail to plan, they will receive whatever life hands them.*

meetings. By giving your children hope and a future, you are imparting family values – which they will in turn duplicate in their own families when they've reached adulthood. In no way have you removed your guardian child's biological parents from your discussion of values. Your child will still seek to gain the approval of their parents, no matter what situation they are in. We all long to have our parents' approval and accolades. You as a guardian may find this hard to accept – but most of you will have to.

Chapter Recap

With this investment of time, you have now created your family values. Having written them out, with timelines to implement them, is a powerful step. In my opinion, there is no greater gift that we can give than this. Remind your children of the importance of core family values, and encourage them with their future life plans. Teaching them this, early on, will be the framework for all of you in making bigger and better life decisions. As I stated in this chapter, it's best to start out with the key areas of life, and then decide what is important in each one. Think of values as boundaries, which establish and shape the framework of a successful life.

Chapter Twenty-Six

Journaling

Let me guess what you're thinking right now: "Scott, are you nuts? I don't have any time, and now you want me to write?" Well, yes, I do want you to write – for many reasons. A journal is a private place, and it allows you space to spread your thoughts out for you (and only you) to see. Allowing your thoughts to flow onto paper is powerful, and it gives you the chance to see them in their simplest form. I have kept a journal for over ten years now, and I have to say that it is second nature for me to write in it regularly. (I actually feel odd if I miss a day!) Now, I don't record the events of the day before (I write in the morning), as I am focused on what is going on in my life in the moment, at that actual time. Not all of the thoughts that come to me are rosy; I often deal with the tough issues in my life. I journaled for four years about writing this book before I ever wrote a draft on the subject of parenting in guardianship. Then, another three years passed before I wrote *Guardian Shift*, the book you are now holding in your hands. I didn't write about anything that you are reading about today; just about how I felt about writing to you in general. Just maybe – I mean *maybe* – I was trying to talk myself out of writing to you. Yes, I tried to talk myself out of doing the whole series of *Guardian Shift* books. That's not the smartest way to get the job done – but it's the truth.

I pleaded with God in my journal, and told Him that he had chosen the wrong guy to write to you. This happened well before I realized what a mistake I'd been making by resisting the process of writing these books for you, to help you in raising your guardian children – or, shall I say, before I obeyed the call to write *Guardian Shift*. Every time I journaled about writing this series, I became more excited – as if it was pulling me into a deeper relationship with the subject, and the encouragement I committed to bring you. Every day I wrote what I was thinking: "I need to do this, and I need to get this information into the hands it is supposed to be in – namely, *yours!"*

Okay – now you've just seen a glimpse of how journaling has shaped my story. Let's talk about how it could help you, in your life, with your guardian child. Here we go… I just found the time to journal, for you, if you are the one saying, "I have no time." If you are a regular attender of "the porcelain throne" in your home – I mean a daily attender – we may have just solved your problem. Now I am talking about adding just a bit more paperwork to your routine. Lock the door – keep everyone out – and you have the perfect excuse for needing more time, and the family won't know any different. I am not saying you should lie – just tell them you are in the middle of your "paperwork," if you get my message. (If you find yourself writing a mini novel, however, I suggest you take your journaling elsewhere!)

Now that we have found you the time to do your writing, it's time for you to get started. First, what should you write about? Well, every one of us has a bit of damage in our lives. This is a good place to start. Because you need to release the toxic waste of your past, I suggest you keep your journal in a private place. Okay, truthfully, you really need to start with a flat-out "garbage dump," as I call it. You have to get rid of the pain – and sometimes writing it out can release it to another dimension. Once you have gone through however many days, or weeks, or maybe even months in the detox mode, we can move on. Next, you can write about the current events with your own child(ren), and your guardian child(ren) as well. Find the areas that they are great in, and be thankful for them. Allow yourself to find the really positive things about your family, and write out what makes each family member so special to you. If anyone in your family is currently giving you problems, you may need to dig hard. Turning your posture toward seeing the positive will eventually help you feel better about yourself, and about every member of your family.

Turning your posture toward seeing the positive will eventually help you feel better about yourself, and about every member of your family.

You will discover that just the daily ritual of allowing the words to flow through you, onto the paper, will be calming once you're done. As you write, listen too – and see what your mind might be trying to tell you. It may have a resolve just waiting for you, or a message of some sort. But if you aren't listening, you will not hear it. You may have to write, and release, and sometimes pause a bit to hear. Journaling will bring clarity to your current day's events, and give you the focus you need to work on all of the tough issues. As you work through them, you can look back through your journal and see the progress you have made. This is valuable. As I have looked back on my own journals, I've seen how my path of writing really helped to resolve the situations I was writing about. Also, while in this "looking back" mode, I found even more insights into various difficult situations. Reflecting is a great exercise. But one cannot reflect on past events if one did not journal about them in the first place. I encourage you to bring out your journal, and get started!

As I transitioned toward more positive journaling, I found many things changing around me. My thoughts changed – and the things around me began to improve. What was *really* happening was that I was changing *me* with my writing – and creating a better attitude. This better attitude allowed me to see things differently. And this is what I desire for you. You may discover that journaling in a positive manner will bring you peace with those current events in your life. It will help you see what you *do* have, and help you to be grateful for it. Is journaling a cure-all? No. It is merely one more tool to help you in your journey through life, and in your guardianship role. It will be healthy for you, and it will be personal. I hope that you will find a friend in your journal, it is and will always be, close to your heart!

Chapter Recap

Writing out your thoughts in a journal is one of many therapeutic ways to find peace. Please take into consideration that you do need to take out the garbage to make room for the good stuff. Just dump the garbage out onto the pages of your journal, and one day you will be rid of it. This will help you recognize the positive things in your life. You will begin to write about them in such a positive way that your spirit will change for the better. I know that what I have outlined here may sound simple as you read it. But I would like to ask you to commit to a sixty-day goal of writing every day. It will become a habit, and you will soon begin to see a difference. Watch what happens when you begin to focus your thoughts on positive outcomes. Your life will change – and circumstances around you may change also!

Chapter Twenty-Seven

Mentoring

Mentoring is one very special way for your guardian child, from "tween" age on up, to find a way to grow. It can provide some really cool insights into the world that they find themselves in. Hopefully, at some point in your life, you were able to take advantage of a mentor in one way or another. I am confident that mentoring can take place all throughout our lives, not just when we are young. Just as a personal trainer teaches you physical training skills, helping you improve your health, a mentor will guide you on life issues. Choosing a mentor to engage with will depend on the specific subject matter involved, much like a personal tutor. For example, many new technological changes have occurred in the last twenty-five years – and let's face it, we're not all on the same learning curve. For this, one would typically need to find a mentor who was younger, and who could really master the technology issues at hand. When this transition took place, I was blessed to have a team of teenagers

> A good mentor, with an eye towards building a great relationship, will ask great questions.

in the house, just at the right time – and I got some great training and mentoring from my own kids. And now that they are grown, I still look to them for help with my more technical stuff.

Let's explore now how your guardian child, from "tween" age on up, could really benefit from a mentor. First, let's discuss your role as a guardian. You're the new sheriff in town – which means that you make the rules the kids have to live by now. This puts you in a huge authority role in their life, and this can create a wall that neither one of you can hurdle when it comes to talking. You, after all, are the protector. When your child needs immediate results in being protected, they will turn to you. But please realize that they may not always open up to you the way they would with a trusted mentor. A quality mentor will become a friend to your child, and earn the child's trust along with the respect required to create a positive relationship. Mentoring should leave a smile on your child's face, and leave them wanting to interact with you. This is the overall goal. It is not easily achieved – and it will take monitoring.

A good mentor should be kind, and should also have awesome listening skills. A mentor will ask questions that will help encourage your child to share about themselves. All of us are hard-wired to open up to people who really care, and we can all tell if they are truly genuine. This is the foundation of the mentor / mentee relationship. Just think about yourself when you meet new people. You don't really ever just want to open up to the person who can't stop talking about themselves, do you? I don't! A good mentor, with an eye towards building a great relationship, will ask great questions. It's like the old saying, that you can only peel an onion one layer at a time. I would add to this, and say you can only peel an onion one layer at a time – because you have to leave room for tears to flow like a river, allowing time to heal and repair before peeling the next layer. This is how much of life is for most of us, in that we need time to heal after an emotional wound.

Mentoring is much more than just having someone for your child to hang out with. A good mentor is a person who will help your child deal with their wounds. The mentor will help the child create a new way of seeing things – and could even become your right-hand person in guiding your child to adulthood. This is the goal here, to raise your guardian child, and eventually to enable them to have a productive life as an adult. Your guardian role will become smoother with a mentor involved. And if it's not, you have the wrong mentor!

Chapter Recap

Mentoring goes back deep into history. You could, once again, use the Bible as an example. Christ worked with His twelve disciples for their time of training. He spent time with them as a group, and individually. We all need someone we can go to who has wisdom to help us through our decisions in life. Having a good mentor can create harmony in your family, as your guardian child finds other safe ways of opening up. This is a solid support system, which ideally will help you shape your child's life. By giving your guardian child an example of making correct choices, you will set them up for success. Go forth and create strong leaders of the generation in your care!

Chapter Twenty-Eight

Language

In this chapter, I want to address language. I don't mean whether you tolerate bad language, or if you speak a second language. What I want to direct you to is the subject of Love Language. According to author Gary Chapman, Ph.D., we all have a love language. I believe that if you have a good understanding of your love language, and that of your family members, all of you will benefit tremendously. Using a person's specific love language shows them how much you value them. I show love to others by complimenting them on what a great job they've done – these are words of affirmation. I would hope, also, to hear praise when I myself did something well. This always makes *me* feel loved. But if I know that your love language is actually about "Acts of Service" – and I do something helpful for you, like run an errand for you or help you clean your garage – you will feel that I'm showing you love. (Don't get your hopes up. I'm not headed to your garage!)

Dr. Chapman has several books on the five "love languages." I believe that they could be helpful resources in raising your natural-born children, as well as your guardian child. My suggestion for you is to read **The Five Love Languages of Children: The Secret to Loving Children Effectively**[1] or **The Five Love Languages of Teenagers: The Secret to Loving Teens Effectively**,[2] depending on the age of your children.

Creating a platform for communicating love to your child is invaluable to you both. Moreover, discovering your guardian child's "love language" could speed recovery time, integration and acceptance into the family by months, if not years. Knowing how to communicate to your child in the language they can hear is an awesome skill to learn. Our nephew's "love language" was acts of service. He was kind and gentle, which made it easy to love him. You could find him cleaning the kitchen after a meal, without our telling him to do so, or working to clean up the patio. These are ways that he knew to show his love for us.

I can remember the times when we just couldn't get a handle on how to communicate with our nephew. His pain was deep and wide, which left him very guarded. The only instinct we had was to keep showing him provision for his well-being. You can think of your own situation, possibly finding several hurts. We just continued to love him, with provision, until the new environment became comfortable for him and he felt he could call it home. Regarding the "honeymoon" phase that I mentioned earlier, we did not even start that for quite a while. We had to navigate our way past the "I don't want to be here" phase. Once life settled in – also known as "he came to his senses" (and I say that in a loving manner!) – our nephew was just fine. He became fun-loving, and playful with all of us. He also became very protective of us – which, I will say, was another way that he communicated his love for us.

It's easy to Google the five "love languages," and learn more specifics than I am giving you here. You can even take an online test to figure out what your own love language is. However you decide to find your child's love language, I recommend that you don't give up. As you know, children are great at seeing whether an adult is sincere

Moreover, discovering your guardian child's "love language" could speed recovery time, integration and acceptance into the family by months, if not years.

in communicating with them – and they can smell the tiniest hint of insincerity. Even if you are simply having a bad day, they can pick up on it. They may take it very personally – and they may think that it's actually about them.

Staying the course in your guardianship journey has, and will continue to have, its difficulties. If you falter in your stamina, in any way, during your guardianship, please seek out one of your support people – or reach out to us on our Facebook or website contact page. We want to help lift you up, and encourage you to stay the course.

Yesterday, before I wrote this section, I went sailing. I learned a bit from Captain Jeff Sparrow (yes, that *is* his real name!) about staying the course. Now, I have only been on a sailboat one other time, nine years ago – so, as you might surmise, I have no skills at all when it comes to sailing. As it happened, we weren't even out of the marina when Captain Sparrow put me in charge of the wheel. YIKES! After I realized he wasn't worried that I'd flip his sailboat over, I began to relax a bit.

We got out into the bay and I learned to keep the sails full of air, which is how we move forward. We were cruising along, and I was worried about staying on course, wanting to go straight toward our destination. I quickly learned that this is not the smartest approach – as sailing is all about using the wind. I pushed the sailboat directly at the goal – and then I lost the wind in my sails, and the boat just stopped. The wind had changed direction, and I wasn't adjusting my course, so we ran out of wind in the sails. It was a great afternoon. And I learned that life is a lot like sailing, in that you have to be ready to make multiple course corrections on the way to your destination.

Chapter Recap

My advice to you here is to continue to make small corrections in your communications until you get it right. If I had done this when I was out sailing, it would have prevented me from stalling the sailboat on the bay – and it also may stop you from falling into patterns of poor communications. Finding that style may take a bit of doing. But once you find it, you will see your child's eyes light up. Love comes in many forms. And we all know how we like to be spoken to, right? Knowing this will give you the insight you need to discover what "love language" your child speaks. Celebrate your successes, and make every moment count. Then be alert to correcting your course – as often as needed – to arrive at your destination!

Chapter Twenty-Nine

Goals — Raising the Bar and Finishing Well

Goals

This can be a fun area for you to explore with the child in your guardianship care, as well as with your natural-born children. You know your own biological children well, so your objective of finding out life directions for them may seem a bit easier. Your child in guardianship, however, could give you a run for your money. The best thing, in my opinion, is to start with the small, short-term goals first. It could be to finish a book that they are reading by a certain day, or to try out for a sport or a play at school. Sit with your guardian child, use a whiteboard or a large sheet of paper (the biggest you can find), and write the child's name right in the middle. Then circle it. (This process is what I have referred to as mind mapping. Please take note here that this really works best for the teenagers in your care. You can be the judge of whether you want to use it with younger children.)

Next, write down some of the things that are most important to your child, in a clockwise rotation, around the main middle circle. These could be dance, baseball, whatever – you get the idea. As you move forward with this, the white space will fill up with one-word targets, and circles around them. I was once told by my writing coach that the words with circles around them allow your subconscious mind to continuously process thought on each topic. This allows a continuing creative flow of thought, and it helps ideas to flow to your conscious mind. So, fill up the white space now, until your mind runs out of life goals that your child may desire, or that you may desire for them. After you are done, you can pull up a chair and stare at the whiteboard or paper to see which goals have a higher priority than others. Remove the lower-level ones, and then begin to question the others and/or refine them into a better form.

Once you have written these one-to-two-word "circle blurbs," you are ready to write them out in a way that will flow from this current time to the time each goal is achieved. Take each word and write out a detailed description, making the desired outcome very clear. For example, one circle could be "basketball" — for this, you would need to describe all the steps your child would need to take in order to achieve this. The one word "basketball" could have different meanings that you might need to discover – it could be that they want to make the team, become better at their current position on the team, or something else. The next step for you is to write out all the steps your guardian child needs to take in order to reach the goal. This will give both of you a clearer picture of what it is that your child wants, and an action plan to get them there. Do this both for short-term and long-term goals.

One thing you should add to the overall list of goals is a plan for moving your guardianship relationship toward adulthood, after your guardian child leaves your home. This is a goal for you to work on, and it may take a separate planning session. This goal says to the child that this time together will come to a close, and that a new beginning will take place. This thought will give your guardian child comfort in that one day they will be fully in charge of their own life. What a great goal to work towards – as we all want, at some point, to be independent, and to run our own lives.

Raising the Bar

"Raising the bar" is a term I'm using to refer to making better choices. It comes from the sport of pole vaulting, where the bar that the athletes vault over keeps getting raised, higher and higher. Each time a competitor clears the bar, the bar is raised again to create an even greater challenge. In this competition, eventually, there is only one person who clears the bar at its highest setting – and this is how a winner is determined. We, as guardians, have the choice to either raise the bar of the situation we may be dealing with – or not. If our situation is one of conflict, we can choose not to react – but instead, to respond with kindness. I am not saying here that I have always taken my own advice very well. Raising the bar is applicable in every situation of life, in that we can always look at our current

As a little reminder, you could simply remember the phrase "Raise the bar" when you are faced with a challenge. This can trigger the act of calmly looking at the whole picture differently.

state and see if we can do better. When we are thrust into a new role, such as caring for other people's children, it's hard not to react. As a little reminder, you could simply remember the phrase "Raise the bar" when you are faced with a challenge. This can trigger the act of calmly looking at the whole picture differently.

Shifting to the new term of raising the bar takes practice. Your guardian child now understands that you both will be observing the choices they make. Their choices can affect the harmony of the family, and if they make poor choices, it becomes a household disturbance. There are so many variables that it would be too difficult to cover the choices themselves. Together, both of you can work on defining their choices and the possible outcomes. It really can help them to mature, and to stabilize their lives, whether they're pulling their new little sister's hair (followed by screams) or sneaking a smoke or a drink of alcohol. Raising the bar can be clear to you and me, but teaching that better choices create better outcomes has some bumps in the road to overcome with your child. You may be silently dealing with hurts, and confidence levels, which affect their choices. Even though they are in a better place now physically, they may not be in a better place mentally. This will affect how they will really understand what you are explaining to them. I love to use a grease board; we have one attached to the wall in the family area. We use it for games, teaching for our eight-year-old, and the "good, better, best" decisions in life. Let me take a moment to define this more. A "good, better, best" decision is when we identify a "good" decision, but then, we move on to finding a "better" one, which may be a stretch. Ultimately, we want to land on the "best" decision for the situation. As before, you can just use a blank piece of paper if you prefer. All of this is similar to what I stated in the Goals section of this chapter.

Let's first work on your guardian child's confidence level, which will lead to how high they decide to raise the bar. If we raise their choices higher for them, it will reveal how comfortable they are with having us help them. Also, it is a barometer of how confident they are with the choice. Once you see that they are out of their comfort zone with the choice, you can help guide them through the process. So many variables will show up, and it is up to you to identify how to help. You have the most difficult task now, of helping your child seek the level of confidence that will bring them to a preferred choice. It could be that they feel they don't deserve it – this is common when they themselves have been treated without regard.

Having teenage boys in our home meant that they had girls and dating on their minds. This seems to be the time when teenagers become the best salespeople of all time. They should be nominated for acting awards for the performances they put on while trying to convince us to go along with them. Of course they will tell you what they want, but it is our job to work it through with them. This is not easy. Making a bad choice in a dating partner, whether you have boys or girls in your home, can affect family harmony adversely. It may be very hard for your guardian child to understand, since they may have come from a dysfunctional home themselves. You have to help them understand that if they settle too easily on a poor choice, it can have a lifetime consequence. You're going to have to fill in the blanks for each time you approach the "let's try harder for a better outcome" topic. Always help them to understand that today's choices affect tomorrow's outcomes.

As you implement the "good, better, best" outcome process, it will become the center point each and every time you sit down together to talk about a decision. They will come to expect that those three components will always be conversation points. When they bring these up before you do, it will be an indication that they are getting it. You will know that it's becoming a habit for them in making good choices – or at least, they're attempting to do this. Let's be honest – we have all had to deal with bad choices, and this helps us to teach our children how to avoid them. Bad choices will come, and how we handle them will tell the child if they can trust you. And when the outcome from the bad choice arises, you have a choice on how to handle it. Take your time in this decision, as it will make or break the future of your open communications. Once your guardian child feels confident that they can bring you any situation and you will walk through it with them without unloading on them, they will bring you every choice to work through first with them – that is, until they are making "best" choices entirely on their own.

In the next book, *Guardian Shift* for Teens, I will be covering the process of "unpacking baggage"; namely, helping teens heal their hurts and insecurities. Then we will look at how to repack their bags for a successful outcome. I can remember that as a child, some of the choices I myself made were not good, and my world fell apart. This was definitely not a good space to be in. My parents worked with me the best they could, and I didn't make it easy for them most of the time. Now, as my life has progressed, I have seen both sides of that coin. I am thankful that I had a few extra second chances, so I recommend that you extend the same courtesy as often as you can to the children in your care.

Finishing Well

"Finishing well" has so many definitions, based upon the objective you wish to achieve. Most of us never set out on a project, or make a choice to do something, and think that we won't finish it, let alone not do it well. We are usually filled with excitement about what we are looking to do or achieve. Most of us never look at our decisions and say, "This is how we will finish" – we just set out on our good idea and do it. It's a battle just to keep going on some things we set out to do. Let's take New Year's resolutions, for example. We may look again at, say, that weight-loss goal, and think, "let's have a great year" – and then we get a month or two down the line and we're caught in a blur. I have read how top business leaders will always create an "exit strategy" in their planning. I know you're saying, "What does business have to do with guardianship?" They have a lot of similar formulas, planning, activities and goals – and the fact that you want to finish well. Your focus is on how to move from whatever situation you and the child in your care are currently in, to a positive one.

Guardianship care is a worthy endeavor and changes the outcome of young lives.

The first thought on your child's mind could be to get their old life back. They may not like the situation they currently find themselves in. You may have a huge power struggle with them, and they may think that being in your care feels like a life sentence. But let's face it, you may feel the same way! While both of you are thinking this, a solution stands ready to be created. You can both sit and talk about how to get to a workable solution for you both, without compromising the position of guardian and authority that you play. Find the "good, better, best" outcome for each topic your guardian child may be going through – and help guide them successfully along their path.

Life is a series of non-stop movement, and you have to know that all situations will come to an end one day. Your guardian child will grow up – they will adjust to their new third-grade teacher, and they will get through all the other obstacles along the way – it's just life. As you outline an action plan to reach the best possible solution, a level of comfort will set in for the subject you're involved in. By directing your focus on finishing well, you will discover the best outcome together. It is not necessarily always going to be the one that pleases both of you, but together you will find a way to develop a desired outcome. The extra effort always has its own benefits, and perseverance has its own reward in the end. I have spent the last seven years working toward getting this book out to you. I have been continually improving the topics, to make them the most relevant I could. It has been a work of joy for me, and I have always sought the highest level I could for you. You are the greatest heroes, as I have previously stated, and I am honored to connect with and serve you.

You are the best thing that has ever happened to the child in your care. Don't become faint hearted! You've got this! Once your support people understand how best to help you, your life will have more and more happy and refreshing moments. As you focus on the best outcome in every area of your life, wait and see how things begin to improve as you set out each and every day to achieve the best with your guardianship. You are the bravest people on the planet to take on the task of raising someone else's child. I know you may feel run over at times, but lift yourself back up. Every time you do, you will become stronger and stronger. You are a warrior who can't be down for long – you are the key to the next generation.

There are many great articles right at your fingertips that relate to finishing well. You will finish, and I believe in you to finish well! Anyone who takes on the task of caring for other people's children is to be commended. Guardianship care is a worthy endeavor and changes the outcome of young lives.

Chapter Recap

With our focus on just getting through the day, it can be hard to find the strength to see into the future. It's not an easy process to sit and create an outcome with a child while they need so many other things in life. Finishing well may be a focus that gives them hope in the here and now, a way to live today on purpose. It is valuable to find a time together and share this reasoning with your guardian child. It gives them something to hope for, and they get to be in control of what they choose. It really is empowering for them to know that they now have a say in their life, versus the way they originally were thrust into your care. So go forth and create the future with them, and find the success that you both deserve.

Section Five

Concluding Thoughts

Parenting children in guardianship is a highly overlooked form of parenting. Building awareness for this form of parenting will help you, and others in your situation – which, in turn, improves the lives of those in your care. As more people around you gain understanding of your shifting family dynamics, the more they will be able to encourage and support you. Finding the sources that best encourage you, and connecting with other guardians in our private Facebook group, will be tremendously valuable to you. Parenting other people's children was never in the structure of our lives from the beginning – but then life happened, or shall I say, life broke down. This left you and me to fill in that gap. Parenting children in guardianship has become more common than one would ever care to believe, but it is the result of a broken society.

Many of us don't have the youthfulness or the finances to handle this new shift in our lives, but we have made huge sacrifices anyway, in order to protect these children. The older you are while parenting children, the more likely you are to be caught in the "generation gap." This is a tough spot to be in, and at my age I have already felt it. It forces you into having to "think younger" to identify with today's younger parents – stretching, to say the least. Ideally, we all raise our own biological children,

Please do share this book, or get copies for those who are close to you, so you can help them understand how they can support you best.

they grow up and life goes on. Unfortunately, we are in a different society today – one in which the family structure has broken down severely – forcing many of us, at all ages, into raising other people's children. Standing in the gap of parenthood for children today are aunts, uncles, cousins, grandparents, great-aunts and -uncles, and really close friends of families from all generations.

Some of you may have already begun downsizing for your retirement years. Now you are ramping up all over again, adding family members to your household and dealing with parenting one more time. My heart goes out to you! Dealing with so many in-laws and out-laws in protecting your child is daunting, to say the least. I hope you connect to our resources, which are there for you so that you can vent, learn, and plug into a community of encouragement. Please feel free to contact us through the Facebook groups, Twitter or my website. I hope you are stronger, now that you have some new tools to work with. It is my hope that you know your all-important place in this new shift. As I have said over and over throughout these pages, *you* are the best person to make a difference. *You* are the one who can do it! Please do share this book, or get copies for those who are close to you, so you can help them understand how they can support you best.

As you go boldly into your guardianship journey, I am confident that you can exercise some or all of the tools laid out in Section Four. Find ways to keep your sanity, regardless, and to communicate with those who are difficult. It is my goal for you to have become stronger as a result of reading the words I have penned to you. You have always been the focus of my thoughts, over the last seven years, as I've been writing this to you. My heart has had you in mind from the moment God seeded the thought of this book series into my head. Since September 8th, 2008, I have stayed the course to bring you this work, to encourage you and those around you. The hurts, the trials and the triumphs I've experienced have all been my inspiration to write to you. The many conversations and emails with guardians have been encouraging to me, and I take each one to heart. If I could speak to each and every one of you reading this book, I would, but for now, social media will have to do. All I claim to know is how much you deserve to have a cheering squad on the sidelines, each and every moment of your journey. May all that I have written here help you accomplish this!

Thank you for investing your time reading **Guardian Shift!**

Section Six

Ways to Connect

Facebook Group — Guardian Shift

Guardians networking together is vitally important for us. We would like to connect as many of you as possible to our Guardian Shift Facebook group. This group is a safe platform for *all* of you who are raising other people's children. The group is a place to vent and ask questions. Everyone is ready to help if they can, even if it's just to say that they hurt right along with you. I also want to invite support people to the group, as they play such a huge role in the well-being of guardians. Their involvement in this group will be beneficial to the families they support, and to the other members as well. More importantly, they will hear from *many* guardians, which will allow them to learn valuable ways to support those who are personally connected to them.

The Guardian Shift Facebook group will have guidelines to adhere to. Let's keep it a safe place to have conversations, and to tell it like it is, without worry. We all need a place to vent, and what better way than to have other guardians from all around the country – and the world, for that matter – to do this with. My wife and I wish we'd had a group like this while we were raising our nephew. If you'd like to become part of the Guardian Shift Facebook group, just head over to www. ScottAmaral.com, click on the Facebook icon and ask to join.

We have moderators who will approve you into the group. Please feel free to introduce yourself, and tell us a bit about your guardian journey.

Guardian Shift Community Page on Facebook

I invite all of you to visit my community page on Facebook. This is a place where we will be posting news, updates and details about upcoming books. We will also be seeking opinions here for future books, cover designs, and other topics of interest.

Twitter

For those of you on Twitter, you can connect with me @Scott_Amaral. Or simply click on the Twitter icon on my website. We will be tweeting often to spread the news of *Guardian Shift*, upcoming books, and current events that relate to raising other people's children. The advent of all this technology has made keeping up to date, and in touch, so very easy.

Instagram

As many of you are aware, a picture can speak a thousand words. Well, Instagram is just the place to do it. You can connect with me at @Scott_Amaral. Here I just do life as I live it. It is a fun platform to share on. I will make sure you get a good diet of encouragement as you keep up with my postings.

Author Website

Another great place to connect with me, on my contact page, is at www.ScottAmaral.com. I invite you to connect with me there as well, and you can email me with your thoughts and comments.

Family Tributes

To my loving wife, Jeannie, I can only say that without you, none of this could have been possible. You have been the finest loving wife and mother any man could ever have asked for. You have spent hours listening to me talk about ***Guardian Shift.*** Your help with layout, subject matter, and hours of reading to make this book possible has been priceless. You have always set a pure example to our sons, daughter, nephew and now our new daughter-in-love, Jennifer. The many nights of reading and re-reading ***Guardian Shift*** are much too many to even count, all to help make this book a blessing to its readers. Thank you! I love you!

To my oldest son Tyler, you are a fine young man. You have always supported helping others, and when it came to helping your cousin, it was no different. You encouraged all of us to keep up the quest of protecting him. You were there to share your friends, family, school and basically, every area of your life, to help him find and become secure in his new life with us. Thank you for sharing – you have a great big heart! Your generous and giving spirit has always been so special to me. You've always been ready to lend me words of encouragement, finding the bright side in every situation. Your creative genius will take you to places that many would only dream of! When it came time for me to buckle down and get *Guardian Shift* written, you cheered me on. Thank you!

To Spencer and Jennifer. To my "social butterfly" middle son. You have been a source of encouragement that has depth beyond words. For always sharing your family and building me up, thank you! God's blessings flowed through your hands as you supported Mom and me through trials that we thought would never end. You were there when words couldn't be spoken, and just sitting with us brought us great comfort. I know that your real-estate career with Keller Williams has flourished beyond that of others with more experience, and it is because of your caring spirit. You have brought us a wonderful daughter-in-love. Thank you! Jennifer, you are so loved, and I am so proud to have you as a part of our family. Thank you for the encouragement you provide to us! I so appreciate your loving spirit and your professional interior design talents. Thank you both!

To Tanner, my fun-loving youngest son – You always make me look at the bright side of every topic. You always pushed me to go out and ride in the buggy around the ranch and have fun with you. Making me buy a much-too-big television when I didn't want to – or just breaking loose and having some fun with me. You have been a shining light to me from the very first day of your life. If I wasn't carrying you on my shoulders, it was in a backpack. You have played such a valuable role in encouraging me toward completing *Guardian Shift.* Thank you!

To Gracie, I thank God for you! The energy you brought into our lives in 2007 has been an ever-flowing and awesome amount of joy. After all these boys, I didn't think I would have ever seen myself doing tea parties. You bring smiles to my soul when you dance with me – and I think the theme song from Frozen is permanently burned into my mind. Thank you!

To my Nephew, I am grateful for our time as your guardian. I saw you grow so much in such a short time. Your many adjustments to a new home and life were remarkable. You always made friends wherever we went. You had a charming smile, at just the right time, always. I am glad you are an adult now – and I always desire the best for you!

To Mom and Dad. First, Dad, I miss you. I know you are with the Lord now. I will always appreciate you for supporting my ventures; you were always my biggest cheerleader. My dear Mother, you have been the glue for our whole family. Your sacrifice to care for Dad during his time of dealing with multiple sclerosis was exemplary; a perfect example of the vows of "for better or worse." You always did it with flair, making the best of it always. Your courage to carry on has burned deep into my soul. Thank you!

Acknowledgments

Dr. Laura Boyd, Ph.D., you have been my cheerleader since 2012. You encouraged me to get this project completed since the first day I met you. Your heart of gold, for the children of this world, shines brightly. I cannot thank you enough for your relentless encouragement and patience while I completed ***Guardian Shift.***

David Rutherford, Dean Rutherford, Jim Corrao and Lito Solorio: The pastoral leadership that all of you provided us at Northside Christian Church in Clovis, California, has been inspiring. We could never have survived our own Guardian Shift years without you. Your encouragement to us to keep going, and your cheering us on, were unprecedented. All of you prayed for us, celebrated our victories and held our hands when things went sideways. Thank you!

Pastor Bill Martin of Calvary Chapel in Puerto Vallarta, Mexico. Your friendship and your teaching of God's word has been so encouraging. My favorite part of the week is going out for tacos with you, and asking deep and challenging questions. You never cease to amaze me with the background and depth that you put into your answers. **Renee Martin,** you are a special friend to us also – Your heart for the many children at the Mission School shows the love of Christ. Bill and Renee, your service as missionaries to the community of Puerto Vallarta has profoundly changed lives. Thank you!

Pastor Blake Gideon of Edmond's First Baptist Church in Edmond, Oklahoma. Thank you for being the spiritual leader I needed while God was ironing out the wrinkles in my life. I will always be grateful to you for walking me through the first chapter of Ephesians. This is where you taught me to obtain my idenity based in God's Word. Your encouragement was appreciated more than words could ever say. Thank you!

Irv and Virginia Brown, you are very persevering grandparents, and guardians, you're an inspiration to me. Both of you stepped up to the plate to raise your grandson at a season in your life when you could have been out on the ocean, cruising around the world. I learned so many things from you, Irv. Your stories of being raised in foster care yourself were sobering and encouraging. They inspired me to push forward on *Guardian Shift*. Thank you!

Tim and Sherrie Lewis, a great big thank you for always standing in the gap for Jeannie and me, and for always seeking the positive side of things. Tim, thank you for always encouraging me to one day write a book. Of course, when you first told me I should, I thought you were crazy, but now I thank you for seeing something in me that I couldn't. *Guardian Shift* is here, in part, because of your encouragement. Thank you!

Clint and Stephanie Fuller, you're like my younger brother and sister. Your love for our family always shines like the bright morning star. You accommodate us at the drop of a hat whenever we are in town. Being with you both is comforting. You now have your own beautiful family of three blessings. You encouraged us at every step of our guardianship. Your support during the writing of **Guardian Shift** has been awesome. Thank you!

Terry and Diane Ashmore, you have seen our family through many great times! I love the hysterical laughter when we get together. Your kindness and encouragement carried us through many trials, and I can't even begin to thank you. Terry, you always kept our lives light-hearted with your silly humor. And your encouragement for us to seek God in all we were doing has been valuable. Diane, for your countless hours of loving counsel, I don't have the words to express my full appreciation. You both are the best! Thank you!

Patrick and Sandy O'Meara, you both supported our guardianship. Sandy, your quick wit, and your way of keeping things real, have always been refreshing to me. Patrick, thanks for pushing me to make sure I would write one or more small-group books so that guardian families could unite during the week. Thank you!

Mike and Deanna Terpening, both of you always listened to us as we needed to vent about life. The fun times out that we shared, and the times when we needed to just sit and talk, were always greatly appreciated. Mike, you always had a way of getting those boys to get moving, and do activities in the youth group. Thank you!

Robert and Anita Ford, you both were so generous to host events at your home for the youth programs. Your park-size yard with a pool created great memories. Anita, your sweet and encouraging spirit was always awesome. Robert, it was always comforting to talk with you, as you have a way of communicating with clear and objective insights. Thank you!

Peter and Melissa Shoenenberger, I thank you both for getting us out on camping trips! We shared many fun outings with our families. The many years of friendship we have enjoyed together is awesome. Hearing us out during our phone conversations, and brightening our day with encouragement during our guardianship and beyond, is highly valued. Thank you!

Vinni and Nancy Smith, where do I start? We have been friends since we were all newly married kids! From the beginning, we knew we would be lifelong friends. You have always made us feel like family. When Jeannie and I ventured around the world on our travels, you took care of everything we needed done while we were away. When I just needed to decompress and be still, you always sent me out to the peaceful koi pond to reflect. How awesome! When our paths separated due to life, and then came back together, it was as if only a day had passed, and we picked up right where we had left off. Everyone needs a Vinni and Nancy in their life! Both of you have encouraged me, as I have labored over ***Guardian Shift,*** with your unwavering support. Thank you!

Bob Papenhausen and Kathleen Clancy Papenhausen, our neighbors, and friends. Living side by side on our little two-and-half acre properties was a blast for us all. The boys loved jumping the fence and swimming in your gigantic swimming pool. Your barbecues were always fun. Seeing the boys off at the end of the driveway made for great conversations and planning sessions. Kathleen, I know Jeannie's favorite part of your park-sized yard was the massive swing set, swinging and talking with you. Thank you!

Mark and Mary Alesia Campbell, I am forever grateful for your belief in me. When I shared my vision of bringing awareness and encouragement to those raising other people's children, you both understood it and became so supportive to me. A big thank you for introducing me to Dr. Laura Boyd, she has been such a blessing to me. Both of you have spoken life into my soul in many ways. I am grateful to call you my friends. Both of you have loved my family from the very first day you met them. Your love and encouragement for my work with Guardian Shift will benefit many lives. Thank you!

Kim Kackman, the best cousin-in-law I could have ever asked for! You have always found a way to cheer us on; always being a friend to us. Your encouragement during our guardianship was tremendously valuable, and as we went up against many obstacles, you supported us. I will never forget your many kind words, and your helping us out when we needed it. Thank you.

Jochen Stratmann, our first teenager. We are so thankful that we responded to the article in the newspaper, "German student needs home for a year." You challenged us in so many ways. We had no clue about parenting teenagers, but you sure taught us. Thank you now for twenty-five-plus years of friendship. The German-engineered closet you built for us, and the endless amount of candy from Europe, are dearly appreciated. Your beautiful wife Miriam, and the two "Exchange Student Grandchildren" you have shared with our family, are so special. Thank you!

A second shoutout to my son Tanner Amaral. Thank you for the countless hours you've spent designing our website, for keeping up with the changes I've made and for the patience you showed when I didn't have a clue what I was asking for. Thank you for getting us into the realm of social media, and ready for a world we knew little of. Most of all, thank you for the crazy number of hours you spent creating the book cover and formatting *Guardian Shift!* It is truly a creation of love, for the purpose of blessing the reader. Thank you!

To my Lord and Savior, Jesus Christ. I stand humbled that you would shape and mold my life, which would ultimately lead me to write *Guardian Shift.* I praise you for being the great physician in my life. You were patient with me when I bucked against you in accepting the call to serve guardians. You tenderly taught me that there is no higher calling than to care for the fatherless – James 1:27. I am truly grateful. Thank you!

Coming Soon in the

Guardian Shift Series

As I looked at introducing this unique series, I felt it would be important to share our direction. In the big picture of building awareness, encouragement and inspiration for all of you guardian warriors, I realized that more attention was needed in presenting various topics of guardianship in an age-appropriate manner. It became clear that I needed to move my attention to the teenagers in your care. All guardians who have teens in their care have the shortest amount of time remaining to guide them successfully into adulthood.

My goal is to introduce books 2, 3 and 4 together. They will work harmoniously as a package, even if you are raising a guardian teen without having any of your own. We will offer the books separately, and as a Trio-Pack. The small-group books which are books 5 and 6, will be introduced last as we progress. Small groups build a great deal of community and support, and we are excited to get these done.

Book 2 – Guardian Shift for the Teen in Guardianship

This book is designed to help the guardian teen integrate into the new world they now find themselves in. It is an in-depth look at bringing some balance into your family's Guardian Shift. This book will give teens in guardianship the advice they need on unpacking the baggage of life. Once they have gone through this process, the book will explore steps they can take on how to repack their bags for success.

Book 3 – Guardian Shift for the Sharing Teen

This book is designed for your own biological teens. They have made room to share their home, their parents, their siblings and their friends. Most of us had to learn how to share our toys, but it is an altogether different story when we are thrust into sharing our lives. In this book, we will acknowledge our teens' generosity and sacrifice, offering ways to hold onto most of what life looked like before guardianship. Then, we will look at the best ways for them to cope with the changes of accommodating the new family member.

Book 4 – Guardian Shift Parent Guide

This book is designed to use in conjunction with both of the teen books, giving you, the guardian parent, some foundational points for working through issues with your teens. The focus of this book in the series is to connect parents and teens so that they can work on topics together, rather than dealing with them separately, which can become explosive. When we are quickly forced into new family roles, life can ignite and throw the whole family dynamics into flames. Teens and adults alike are typically not prepared for this new Guardian Shift. The Parent Guide will assist parents in identifying issues with their teens, offering supportive insights to lay a new and positive foundation. This guide is fully interactive, and the subjects the teens are reading in their own books will allow all parties to be on the same page for open discussion. The theme of this book will focus on how to finish well. It opens up the perspective of looking towards a time in the future, which will come when the relationship has transitioned into adulthood.

Book 5 – Guardian Shift for the Small Group

This small-group book is focused on building relationships and encouragement in small-group settings. Families need fellowship, especially with others in similar circumstances of raising children in guardianship. The vision for the Small-Group book set is for community and faith-based organizations alike to offer this as a way for families to connect. Parenting in guardianship is a lonely and isolated path, and small groups are powerful in building relationships and relief for guardians.

Book 6 – Guardian Shift
Small Group Leaders Guide

The leaders guide is designed to help participants as they meet together and go through their small-group book. The leader will help facilitate building relationships and encouragement in small-group settings. If the leader is not personally involved with parenting in guardianship, this guide will help them to learn the real-life struggles that guardians go through, and to lead the group through the challenges they are facing.

Guardian Shift Children's Books

My wife Jeannie is presenting some key topics of guardianship through her children's books, which focus on children ages four to seven in guardianship care. The books will come with fun images, and story lines. Jeannie's books will address the changes and challenges that the children are facing. Her goal is to help with integration and creating family ties. We intend to introduce the series for all of the grandparents, aunts, uncles, and anyone raising those little angels. Jeannie has a huge heart for the little ones in your care.

Notes

INTRODUCTION

1. Grandfacts http://www.aarp.org/relationships/
   friends-family/grandfacts-sheets/

CHAPTER TWO - MILLIONS ARE ON
                    THIS JOURNEY

1. Grandfacts http://www.aarp.org/relationships/
   friends-family/grandfacts-sheets/
2. http://www.aarp.org/relationships/friends-family/
   info-09-2011/grandrally-raising-grandkids.html
3. http://www.un.org/esa/socdev/family/docs/IDF-
   2013DONNABUTTS.pdf
4. Ibid.

CHAPTER EIGHT - GRANDPARENT GLUE

1. Makin, C. (2014) 'More Grandparents Raising Their Grandkids', Courier News. Available at: http://www.usatoday.com/story/news/
   nation/2014/07/26/more-grandparents-rais-
   ing-their-grandkids/13225569/ (Accessed: 23
   January 2015)

CHAPTER NINE - WOW! A HANDFUL

1. Grandfacts http://www.aarp.org/relationships/ friends-family/grandfacts-sheets/

CHAPTER 13 - ENCOURAGING SOURCES

1. Bible (NIV) Jeremiah 29:11

CHAPTER 23 - HOLLYWOOD AND BEYOND

1. Bible (NIV) Esther 2:7
2. One Night With The King (2006) Directed by Michael O. Sajbel [Film]. USA: Gener8Xion Entertainment.
3. https://en.wikipedia.org/wiki/One_Night_with_ the_KingHeidi (1937) Directed by Allan Dwan [Film]. USA: Twentieth Century Fox Film Corporation.
4. Rebecca of Sunnybrook Farm (1938) Directed by Allan Dwan [Film]. USA: Twentieth Century Fox Film Corporation.
5. Bright Eyes (1934) Directed by David Butler [Film]. USA: Fox Film Corporation.
6. The Fresh Prince of Bel-Air (1990-1996) Warner Bros. Television
7. You can watch this scene on YouTube at https:// www.youtube.com/watch?v=GmerFuzRNZ4
8. Ruby & the Rockits (2009) ABC Family Worldwide
9. The Beverly Hillbillies (1962-1971) CBS Television Network

CHAPTER 28 - LANGUAGE

1. Chapman, G & Campbell, R. *The 5 Love Languages of Children: The Secret to Loving Children Effectively* Northfield Publishing; Reissue edition (May 1, 2016)
2. Chapman, G. *The 5 Love Languages of Teenagers: The Secret to Loving Teens Effectively* Northfield Publishing; Reissue edition (May 1, 2016)

About the Author

Scott Amaral was born and raised in the heart of the Central Valley of California. He married the love of his life, Jeannie, in 1983 and together they have raised three sons: Tyler, Spencer and Tanner. In 2007, they were also blessed with a late in life surprise which has them currently raising a sweet daughter, Gracie. Together they have devoted their lives to making an investment in youth. Starting in 1990, they began hosting exchange students from Germany, Sweden and Japan. In 2003 they became guardians to their nephew, which started their journey to bring you *Guardian Shift*.

Made in the USA
San Bernardino, CA
25 September 2016